Monitoring poverty and social exclusion 2006

Monitoring poverty
and social exclusion 2006

Guy Palmer, Tom MacInnes and Peter Kenway

JOSEPH ROWNTREE
FOUNDATION

np institute
new Policy
poverty.org.uk

The **Joseph Rowntree Foundation** has supported this project as part of its programme of research and innovative development projects, which it hopes will be of value to policy makers, practitioners and service users. The facts presented and views expressed in this report are, however, those of the author[s] and not necessarily those of the Foundation.

Joseph Rowntree Foundation
The Homestead
40 Water End
York YO30 6WP
Website: www.jrf.org.uk

ISBN-13: 9781859355350
ISBN-10: 1859355358

A pdf version of this publication is available from the JRF website (www.jrf.org.uk).

A CIP catalogue record for this report is available from the British Library.

Designed by Adkins Design
Printed by Alden Group Ltd

Further copies of this report, or any other JRF publication, can be obtained either from the JRF website (www.jrf.org.uk/bookshop/) or from our distributor, York Publishing Services (Tel: 01904 430033).

Contents

Introduction

The *Monitoring poverty and social exclusion* series

This is the ninth in a series of annual reports which began in 1998 with the aim of providing an independent assessment of the progress being made in eliminating poverty and reducing social exclusion in Britain. This report follows the previous ones in all essential respects, namely:

- There are 50 indicators each comprising two graphs. The first graph typically shows progress over time while the second shows how the problem varies between different groups within the population, divided variously according to either income level, social class, economic or family status, gender, ethnicity etc.

- The indicators are grouped into themes and the themes into six chapters. Four of the chapters are focused on particular age groups within the population, namely children, young adults aged under 25, adults aged 25 to retirement and adults above retirement. In addition, there is an opening chapter on the subject of income and a closing one on the subject of community.

These reports are only one part of the output of *Monitoring poverty and social exclusion* and there are also separate reports for Scotland (2006), Wales (2005) and Northern Ireland (2006).

www.poverty.org.uk

In their turn, the indicators in these reports are themselves only a small subset of the complete set of indicators which have been created as part of this project, all of which are available on the project website www.poverty.org.uk. At the last count, the website contained more than 750 graphs and around 50 maps, drawing on a combined databank some 40Gb in size.

Anybody interested in any of the material in this report should, if they wish to explore further, visit the website. Anybody wishing to reproduce material from the report is also encouraged to visit the website to check that there is not more up-to-date information or later version of a graph. While the reports come out annually, the graphs on the website are updated within a few weeks of the data being published. The data behind every graph is also available on the website.

Any use of this material should be acknowledged using the following text: 'www.poverty.org.uk, published by the New Policy Institute on behalf of the Joseph Rowntree Foundation'.

The geographical scope of the report

Wherever data sources permit, the scope of this report is the United Kingdom, that is England, Wales, Scotland and Northern Ireland. In some cases, however, only analysis at a Great Britain level (i.e. not including Northern Ireland) is possible. Furthermore, in a few cases, even the data from England, Scotland and Wales is not comparable and, in such cases, the analysis is either for England and Wales or for England only.

Commentary

Introduction and overview

This is the ninth edition of *Monitoring poverty and social exclusion*. The first one, published in 1998 and subtitled *Labour's Inheritance*, documented the poverty and social exclusion that confronted the government that came to office the year before. This edition, which gives an account of the position in 2006, can perhaps be thought of as documenting Tony Blair's legacy. Against that background, this commentary draws a number of higher level conclusions about what the analysis in this report shows has happened over the last nine years.

In the case of child poverty, taking stock in this way is especially timely since the latest available income statistics are for the year when the government's first milestone on the road to abolishing child poverty was due to be reached. Although there had been considerable progress, that target, to reduce child poverty by a quarter, was not reached. The first question we therefore address in this commentary is 'why?' The rest of the discussion is arranged under five headings. Along with child poverty, the headings and the main conclusions from each are as follows:

- ■ **Poverty among children**. Child poverty has come down significantly, but when half of the children still in poverty are living in families that are doing paid work, the key proposition behind the government's strategy, that 'work is the route out of poverty' cannot be true for many people. Unless the scale of in-work poverty can be reduced, future substantial reductions in child poverty are very unlikely.

- ■ **Poverty among adults**. The big fall in poverty among pensioners, especially single pensioners, has been a major success of the anti-poverty strategy. By contrast, the failure to reduce poverty among working-age adults has been a major weakness. In-work poverty is one part of this; what 'security' should mean for working-age people who are not in work is the other.

- ■ **Inequalities in income and pay**. Despite the fall in poverty, three-quarters of the extra income created over the last decade has gone to richer households. While gender pay inequality has fallen, especially at the bottom, higher earnings have grown proportionately faster than the average. Overall earnings inequalities are therefore widening and the beliefs that sustain them remain unchallenged.

- ■ **Health inequalities**. Health inequalities by social class are pervasive, though the scale varies a lot from subject to subject. What limited up-to-date information is available shows health inequalities to be more impervious to change than other forms of inequality. The challenge remains to find explanations for them that contain the possibility of policy intervention.

- ■ **Minimum educational standards**. Progress in the numbers reaching 'headline' standards at age 11 and 16 diverts attention from the failure to improve outcomes for the quarter of 19-year-olds who fail to reach a minimum educational standard. Since these people face the highest risk of poverty in adult life, this is a sign that one of the major causes of future poverty is not being addressed.

- ■ **Exclusion by institutions**. In a number of areas, from bank accounts to central heating, exclusion has fallen substantially where government has taken a stand. Yet there remain many others, perhaps above all in the workplace, where people at the bottom are the least likely to benefit from support and services that are on offer. Government, employers and trade unions are all in part responsible.

Most of these conclusions involve a mixture of the positive and the negative, often strongly so. With the possible exception of health inequalities, they also all suggest that, once government identifies something as important, progress can be expected to follow. This shows just how important it was that government took up the cause of poverty and social exclusion after 1997 because little of the progress since then would have been achieved without it. It also shows how important it is that the government continues to accord a high priority to these subjects in the future.

This is not to say, however, that all that is needed is a continuation of the current approach. In particular, we believe that the guiding principles of the anti-poverty strategy now need urgent review, partly because they are so at odds with reality (the extent of in-work poverty) and partly because their meaning has never been developed for a key group (working-age adults without work). Equally seriously, the failure to make any progress in reducing the number of older teenagers lacking minimum qualifications suggests that one of the root causes of tomorrow's poverty, namely worklessness and/or low paid, low productivity work, is not yet being addressed.

Finally, there needs to be a decisive break with the idea that poverty and social exclusion can be reduced, never mind eliminated, through government action alone. The record since 1997 does not provide many examples of where other institutions have made a difference but there are some. Rather than just calling for direct action by central government, it might be a useful discipline if those committed to ending poverty also turned their attention to the many other institutions with a role to play, beginning, we would suggest, in the workplace.

> ## The current measurement of income poverty
>
> A household is defined as being in income poverty ('poverty' for short) if its income is less than 60 per cent of the contemporary Great Britain median household income. In 2004/05, the latest year for which data is available, this was worth £100 per week for a single adult with no dependent children, £183 per week for a couple with no dependent children, £186 per week for lone parents with two dependent children and £268 per week for a couple with two dependent children.
>
> These sums of money are measured after income tax, council tax and housing costs have been deducted, where housing costs include rents, mortgage interest, buildings insurance and water charges. The sum of money left over is therefore what the household has available to spend on everything else it needs, from food and heating to travel and entertainment.

Poverty among children

Progress towards the child poverty target

The latest official figures on child poverty are for the year (2004/05) when the first milestone on the road to abolishing child poverty was due to have been passed, namely to reduce child poverty by a quarter compared with 1998/99.

What the figures show is that this target was not reached whichever measure of income poverty is used. On the more commonly used 'after deducting housing costs' measure, the number of children in poverty in Britain fell by 700,000, or 17 per cent, from 4.1 million in 1998/99 to 3.4 million in 2004/05. On the alternative 'before deducting housing costs' measure, the proportional fall was greater, at 23 per cent, but still slightly short of the target. [8A][1]

The only way to characterise what has been achieved so far is surely 'mixed': on the one hand, steady and solid progress, unequivocally reversing what had been a long upward trend in child poverty beginning at least as long ago as the end of the 1970s; on the other, equally unequivocally, falling short of a target that itself is still a long way from the eventual goal of abolition.

What lies behind the fall in child poverty?

Other studies have looked at what policies could be followed in order to continue to make progress in reducing child poverty.[2] The focus here, by contrast, lies in understanding why and how child poverty has come down, as well as why it has not actually come down further already.

Table 1 summarises the statistics on the poverty status of children in 1998/99, the base year chosen by the Government against which to measure progress, and 2004/05, with the information shown separately according to the work status of their family.[3]

Table 1

	1998/99	2004/05
Children in working families, of which:	10.0m (79%)	10.2m (81%)
■ in poverty	2.0m (16%)	1.7m (14%)
■ not in poverty	8.0m (63%)	8.5m (68%)
Poverty 'risk'	20%	17%
Children in workless families, of which:	2.6m (21%)	2.4m (19%)
■ in poverty	2.1m (17%)	1.7m (14%)
■ not in poverty	0.5m (4%)	0.7m (5%)
Poverty 'risk'	80%	72%
All children, of which:	12.6m (100%)	12.5m (100%)
■ in poverty	4.1m (33%)	3.4m (27%)
■ not in poverty	8.5m (67%)	9.1m (73%)
Poverty 'risk'	33%	27%

The first point is that all the key measures moved in the right direction. In particular:

- ■ The number of children in working families went up (from 10 million to 10.2 million) while the number in workless families went down (2.6 million to 2.4 million).

- ■ The number of children in poverty went down both among working families (2 million to 1.7 million) and workless ones (2.1 million to 1.7 million).

- ■ The risk of poverty (that is, the proportion of children in poverty) also went down among both working families (20 per cent to 17 per cent) and workless ones (80 per cent to 72 per cent).

The second point is that most of the fall in child poverty has been due to the reduced risks for both working and workless families rather than from the shift into work. More specifically:

- ■ If the proportion of children who are in workless families had remained at its 1998/99 level of 21 per cent, the reduced poverty risks would have led to a 0.5 million reduction in child poverty to 3.6 million (12.5 x (0.21 x 0.72 + 0.79 x 0.17)).

■ By contrast, if those risks had remained at their 1998 level, the drop in worklessness would have led to a reduction in child poverty of only 0.2 million to 3.8 million (12.5 x (0.19 x 0.80 + 0.81 x 0.20)).

Since the driving forces behind these reduced risks – tax credits, benefit reform and the minimum wage – are also likely to have been one of the causes of the fall in worklessness, they are clearly of central importance.

Why has the progress not been greater?

So why was the child poverty target missed? The first possibility is that the number of children who are in workless families did not fall fast enough. It is certainly true that, while reducing that number has long been a government priority, there are still more children in that situation in the UK than anywhere else in the European Union. [10B] In fact, however, the number of children in workless households has been falling for a decade [10A], while employment among lone parents (who account for two-thirds of all children in workless poverty [8B]) has risen sharply, from 0.9 million in 1997 to 1.3 million in 2006.[4] [28A] While a bigger fall in worklessness would have helped, it is not clear how much more could actually have been expected given the progress there has been.

The second possibility is that the reforms to the tax credits and benefits somehow did not help enough families out of poverty. Tax credits are certainly not just for families in poverty. [9B] Even so, we estimate that the number of children in working families taken out of poverty by the money received from tax credits was, at 1.1 million in 2004/05, 0.8 million higher than the number lifted out of poverty by the predecessor to tax credits in 1998/99. [9A] Combined with the fall in workless poverty, a fall in in-work poverty of 0.8 million would have been enough to have achieved the target.

The reason why it was *not* enough is that, over the same period, the total number of children in working families who were either in poverty despite tax credits, or would have been in poverty but for the credits, increased from 2.3 million in 1998/99 to 2.8 million in 2004/05. [9A] It is this increase which explains why 0.8 million children can be taken out of in-work poverty while the total number of children in in-work poverty falls by only 0.3 million.

In summary, then, although the number of children in workless families has gone down, and although tax credits are helping many more children in working families out of poverty, the immediate reason why the child poverty target was missed was because the number of children needing help to escape poverty has gone up too.

The numbers needing tax credits to escape poverty are new estimates and therefore subject to more than usual uncertainty. But whatever the precise increase may be, the deeper issue is the sheer scale of the underlying problem of in-work poverty. Table 1 makes this quite clear: half of all the children in poverty in 2004/05 (1.7 million) belonged to working families, a similar proportion to that in 1998/99. Unlike workless families in poverty, the great majority (80 per cent) of children in in-work poverty are in two parent families rather than lone parent ones. [8B]

In our view, it is a failure to recognise the extent of in-work poverty that is the fundamental threat to the child poverty strategy. Indeed, as a statement of fact, the crucial proposition that work is the route out of poverty cannot be true when in-work poverty accounts for half of all child poverty. Yet if the strategy is to succeed, the proposition needs to become true. For that to happen, in-work poverty needs to be brought clearly to public attention, and a debate begun about who is responsible for it. The evidence of the past few years suggests that simply trying to compensate for it by giving people tax credits is unlikely to provide a sustainable, long-term solution.

Summary of key points

1. 700,000 fewer children are now in income poverty than in 1998/99, a fall of 17 per cent. On the alternative 'before deducting housing costs' measure, the fall is 23 per cent. The government's target for this period was for a fall of 25 per cent. [8A]

2. Half the children in poverty have someone in their family doing paid work. Of these, four-fifths live with two parents. Among the half of children in poverty who are in workless families, two-thirds live with just one parent. [8B]

3. Tax credits now help more than a million children in working households out of poverty, but the number needing such help has risen sharply. [9A]

4. Although the number of children who are in workless households has fallen by a quarter over the last decade, the UK still has a higher proportion than any other EU country. [10A], [10B]

Poverty among adults

Substantial falls in pensioner poverty

Pensioner poverty gets much less media attention than child poverty, presumably because there is no government target for it. Yet the record on pensioner poverty has in fact been extremely good, with the pensioner poverty rate falling rapidly, from 27 per cent in the late 1990s to 17 per cent in 2004/05.[3A] Pensioners now account for just one in six of all the people in income poverty.[3B] The pensioner poverty rate, which used to be almost as high as the rate for children, is now slightly lower than that for working-age adults. As a result, poverty is now no longer something that should be associated particularly with pensioners.

The improvement that has taken place for single pensioners has been even greater than this. In the late 1990s, the poverty rate for single pensioners was 33 per cent, equal to that for children. In the six years since then, the rate has halved, and is now no different from that for pensioner couples. The rate for couples is also lower than it was, though the fall there, from around 23 per cent to 17 per cent, only began two years ago. Over such a short period, that too is a very rapid rate of decline. [38A]

There can also be no doubt that what brought about this dramatic improvement was the introduction of the Pensioner Minimum Income Guarantee in 1999 and the revamped and extended version of this – Pension Credit – in 2003. Means-tested benefits such as these do not address the root of the problem, but when they are used as they have been here, as a vehicle for delivering big increases in benefits to those with the lowest incomes, they can have rapid effects.

The future measurement of income poverty

In the period to 2004/05, both the government and its critics used the same main threshold of income poverty when assessing progress towards the government's child poverty targets, namely a household income of 60 per cent of the contemporary Great Britain median household income. For the period to 2010, however, the government is planning to use a more complicated set of measures. The major changes are threefold, namely:

- Explicit adoption of incomes 'before deducting housing costs', whereas the previous practice was either to look at incomes 'after deducting housing costs' or both before and after.

- The inclusion of a fixed income threshold, uprated by inflation only, as well as the relative threshold which rises as society becomes richer over time.

- The inclusion of material deprivation measures, which look at the proportion of the population who 'lack because they cannot afford' a defined set of items and activities which are deemed to be essential in contemporary society.

While each of these measures provides valuable information, it is not yet clear precisely how the government plans to use them to judge progress. Given that the measures may well move in different directions over time, this could lead to potential confusion and disagreement about how much progress is being achieved.

A number of specific, potential concerns also arise, each of which is discussed below.

In broad terms, the **before and after deducting housing cost measures** show similar trends over time.[2A] Rather, the concern here is with the perceived geographic variations in poverty, particularly the perceived levels of poverty in areas with high housing costs. For example, London has a very high poverty rate using the after deducting housing costs measure but only an average poverty rate using the before deducting housing costs measure.[2B] A major reason for this is that, in the before deducting housing costs measure, Housing Benefit is counted as household income so households in receipt of Housing Benefit are considered to have a much higher income than the actual money which is available to them. This can also lead to potentially perverse implications for policy. For example, if social housing rents were raised, and Housing Benefit increased to compensate, this would lead to reductions in the numbers judged to be in poverty even though no one was better off as a result.

The main issue with **fixed thresholds** is how the government uses them to judge progress. As society becomes richer, a fixed threshold always follows a much better trend than a relative threshold. Indeed, the number of people below a fixed threshold did not rise during the 1980s, even though this is a period when it is widely agreed that poverty got a lot worse.[1A] So, whereas an upward future trend would clearly be very bad news, it is not clear how a downward trend should be interpreted.

The issue with **material deprivation measures** is their reliability as an objective measure given that they have (at least until now) been based on people's subjective views as to whether or not they can afford a particular item/activity. So, for example, on the first year that such data was collected (2004/05), it showed that, while many people on low incomes said that they cannot afford selected essential items, so did quite a lot of people on average incomes. [5A]

That said, material deprivation measures certainly provide some insights. For example, they suggest that a lack of consumer durables, clothes or appropriate food are only relatively small parts of the problem. By contrast, a much bigger part of the problem is those households who lack (because they cannot afford them) items and activities that can be described as directly money-related. What these figures suggest is that, instead of an image marked by a lack of *things*, modern poverty is marked by real difficulties in paying for essential services, or accumulating small financial assets (pensions, savings, insurance, a bank account) or taking part in activities (like going on holiday once a year) that the rest of society takes for granted. [5B]

Stagnation in working-age poverty rates

In contrast to the great improvement in pensioner poverty, the 19 per cent poverty rate among working-age adults has barely changed for at least a decade. [3A] At 6.2 million, the number of working-age adults in poverty is now more than pensioner and child poverty combined and more than half of these do not have dependent children. [3B]

While the poverty rate among working-age adults has remained unchanged, there have been big changes in their division between working and workless households. For example, the number of adults aged 25 to retirement who are both in poverty and in workless households has fallen from 2.5 million to 2.1 million over the last decade. By contrast, the number who are in poverty but in working households has risen from 1.3 million to 1.9 million. As a result, nearly half of all adults age 25 to retirement in poverty now live in working households whereas, a decade ago, only one third did. [23B]

Working-age disabled adults are especially at risk: 30 per cent of disabled adults aged 25 to retirement are now in poverty, twice the rate for non-disabled adults. This is not only twice the rate for non-disabled adults but is also higher than a decade ago. [24A] The main reason for this high poverty rate is that the majority are not in paid work. [28A] Yet it is also clear that disabled people face formidable barriers in finding work. The most striking evidence of this is that graduates with a work-limiting disability have a higher chance of being out of, but wanting, work than a non-disabled adult who has no qualifications at all. [28B] Neither a willingness to work, nor self-improvement through education, are therefore sufficient to give disabled adults anything like the same economic prospects as their non-disabled peers.

What lies behind the failure to reduce working-age poverty? It cannot simply be the lack of a target because there has never been a target for pensioner poverty either. As with child poverty, part of the explanation is that the scale of the problem of in-work poverty has not been fully acknowledged, with the result that one of the two key premises of the strategy, namely 'work for those who can', is seriously at odds with the evidence. But as that observation applies to child poverty too (where the rate *has* come down), in-work poverty cannot be the sole reason why the adult poverty rate has not fallen.

Rather, we suggest that an additional reason is that it has never been clear what the other key premise of the government's anti-poverty strategy, namely 'security for those who cannot (work)' is supposed to mean for working-age people. Two specific questions need answering: first, who counts as being 'unable' to work; and second, what would constitute 'security' for them? For pensioners, there are clear answers to both questions, namely, 'all of them' and 'a level of state support close to, or above, the poverty line'. For pensioners, these answers have provided a basis for policy, something which is still lacking in the case of working-age adults.

What the answers to these two questions should be for working-age adults is beyond our scope here. But it is noticeable that government policy towards out-of-work benefits for working-age adults remains the same as that inherited from its Conservative predecessor, namely, that the value of such benefits should go up only in line with prices. As a result, whereas benefits for households with children and for pensioner households have either risen relative to earnings, or at least held their own, benefits for working-age adults without dependent children are now worth 20 per cent less relative to earnings than in 1997 – and are far below the poverty line. [6A]

Summary of key points

5. The poverty rate for pensioners has come down from 27 per cent in the late 1990s to 17 per cent in 2004/05. Among single pensioners, the rate has halved over the period, from 33 per cent to 17 per cent. Pensioners now account for just one sixth of all the people in poverty. [3A], [38A], [3B]

6. The poverty rate for working-age adults remains unchanged at 19 per cent. Nearly half of working-age adults in poverty live in households where someone is doing paid work. [3A], [23B]

7. At 30 per cent, the poverty rate for disabled adults is twice that for non-disabled adults, a difference markedly higher than a decade ago. The main reason for this high poverty rate is the high levels of worklessness. Indeed, a graduate with a work-limiting disability is more likely to be lacking but wanting work than an unqualified person with no disability. [24A], [28B]

8. Relative to earnings, out-of-work benefits for working-age adults are now worth 20 per cent less than in 1997. [6A]

Inequalities in income and pay

Low pay and pay inequalities

The link between low pay and income poverty is a complex one, chiefly because it is individuals who are paid whereas it is households whose incomes are counted for the purposes of measuring poverty. For a variety of reasons, the great majority of low paid workers do not live in households that are deemed to be in poverty. These reasons include working long hours, living with others who also work and, of course, the additional money that is now available via tax credits. But even though most low paid workers are not in poverty, it remains the case that the majority of workers whose households are in poverty *are* themselves low paid: low pay is therefore a major cause of in-work poverty.[5]

Our evidence shows that the proportion of people who are low paid, defined here as £6.50 an hour in 2005,[6] has been coming down slowly since 2000. This is particularly so for women, where the proportion (among women aged 22 plus) fell from 37 per cent in 2000 to 29 per cent in 2005. The proportion of men age 22 plus who were low paid also fell, from 17 per cent to 14 per cent. While there is still a big gap between men and women, it has narrowed. [30A]

Among full timers, there are equal numbers of low paid men and low paid women. The reason why there are many more low paid women overall is because there are many more women doing low paid part-time work. [30B] Part-time work carries a high (50 per cent) risk of low pay. However, as that risk is actually the same for men and women, it would seem that it is the low pay of part-timers, rather than the low pay of women, that is the immediate problem. [32B]

There is also some evidence of a reduction in pay inequalities between low paid men and women in full-time employment. Using a different definition of low pay, a low paid woman in 2005 earned 50 per cent of median male earnings, up from 47 per cent a decade ago.[7] Over the same period, a comparable low paid man continued to earn 55 per cent of median male earnings. As a result, although there is still a gap between low paid male and female earnings, it is only two-thirds of what it was a decade ago. [32A] For those with below average earnings, therefore, inequality *between* men and women has fallen, while inequality *among* men (and *among* women) has stayed the same.

What about those with above average earnings? Here, using an analogous definition of a high paid worker, the gender pay gap has also come down. The gap is, however, still larger than for low paid workers, and it has also come down by less. What really stands out about upper half earnings is that both high paid men and high paid women have moved ahead relative to male median earnings, up from 160 per cent to 175 per cent for women, and up from 205 per cent to 217 per cent for men. [32A] In summary therefore, for those with above average earnings, while inequality *between* men and women has fallen, inequality among men (and *among* women) has risen.

Some of the credit for the fall in gender inequality among low paid workers must belong to the minimum wage, both directly and in the signal it sends about the unacceptability of very low pay. The longstanding demand for equal pay for women may also have contributed to the smaller but widespread fall in gender pay inequality. But clearly this has not translated into reduced pay inequality more generally, especially in higher earnings.

Income inequalities

On the face of it, the picture of what has happened to net household incomes is very different from the picture for gross, individual earnings. Here, the evidence shows that the incomes of households with below average incomes have usually seen *larger* real term percentage increases (that is, after inflation) than households with above average incomes. More specifically, households with below average incomes have enjoyed real increases of between 35 per cent and 40 per cent over the last decade whereas those with above average incomes have had increases of around 30 per cent. [4A]

There are, however, two important exceptions to this picture, at the bottom (where the incomes of the poorest tenth have gone up by only 25 per cent) and at the top (where the incomes of the richest tenth have gone up by 40 per cent). Taking these into account, overall inequality, as measured using the Gini coefficient, has remained largely unchanged.[8]

It is important to remember, however, that the only basis on which it is possible to argue that overall income inequality is unchanged is by referring to *proportional changes* in income rather than *absolute amounts*. If one looks at the absolute amounts that households have gained over the past decade after allowing for inflation, a very different picture emerges. Now the pattern is that the higher the household income, the bigger the increase, for example £60 a week extra for households in the third decile but £100 a week extra for those in the eighth. Outcomes at the bottom and the top are even more extreme: £10 a week and £320 a week respectively. [4A] As a result, three-quarters of the increase in income over the last decade has gone to households with above average incomes, and a third has gone to households in the richest tenth.

The use of ratios and proportions to express inequality and poverty ('60 per cent of median income') is in our experience both universal and taken for granted. But an unthinking belief that uniform *percentage* increases in income are the mark of fairness is one of the ideas that sustains inequality in this country. If one believes that it is absolute amounts that matter, then the story over the last decade is a very different one and much more adverse.

Summary of key points

9. The proportion of workers aged 22+ who are low paid (£6.50 an hour in 2005) has fallen from 37 per cent in 2000 to 29 per cent in 2005 for women and from 17 per cent to 14 per cent for men. Though still substantial, the pay gap between men and women has narrowed at every level of pay, though more so at the bottom. [30A]

10. Apart from a slight but general fall in gender pay inequality, pay at the bottom has moved in line with average pay over the last decade while pay at the top has gone up faster. [32A]

11. Except for households in the top and bottom tenths, households with below average incomes have enjoyed bigger proportional increases over the last decade than households with above incomes. In terms of the extra money, however, three-quarters has gone to those with above average incomes, and a third has gone to those in the richest tenth. [4A]

Health inequalities

The relevance of health to a report on poverty and social exclusion lies in the extent to which those who are disadvantaged in other ways suffer worse health outcomes than others.

The evidence on the link between health inequalities and deprivation, usually measured by social class, shows them to be pervasive. In other words, the risk of suffering from a particular health problem is greater for people from manual backgrounds (or with lower income) than for those from non-manual backgrounds. This is true for children with a low birthweight [11A], infant death [12A], child tooth decay [12B], teenage motherhood [13B], young adult suicides [22B], premature death for reasons of heart disease or lung cancer [35B], limiting long-standing illness [36B] and risk of mental ill-health among people of working-age [37B]. The one exception to this pattern is limiting long-standing illness among those age 75 and above where the differences by social class, still visible for those between 65 and 74, have almost disappeared: nature at last has caught up. [41B]

Although health inequalities are to be found everywhere, they vary a lot in size. At its smallest, (low birthweight, infant death, tooth decay, premature death due to heart disease), the degree of inequality is between a third and a half higher. At its greatest, the ratio can be three to one (young adult suicides) or even nine to one (teenage motherhood). In all the adult health indicators, there are also marked differences between men and women, although nowhere do they swamp the underlying class differences.

Where information over time is available (low birthweight babies, infant death), there is no sign that these inequalities are coming down. In general, however, information over time is sparse and difficult to obtain, in marked contrast with all the other areas covered in this report. It should also be pointed out that the difficulties in obtaining data are usually greater for England than for Scotland, Wales or Northern Ireland.

The best that can be said is that, in a number of cases, the underlying statistic has been trending downwards for the population as a whole, notably for premature deaths [35A], young adults suicides [22A] and, possibly, underage pregnancies [13A].

The lack of any evidence that health inequalities are coming down is not for want of government targets. In our view, the issue is whether there are yet any adequate explanations for these inequalities which would form a sound basis for policy intervention. Until there is, the inequalities are likely to continue, registering the effects of the many factors that influence them.

Summary of key points

12. Health inequalities associated with class, income or deprivation are pervasive and can be found in all aspects of health, from infant death and the state of children's teeth to the risk of mental ill-health. The limited information on progress over time (infant death, low birthweight) shows no sign that they are shrinking. [11A], [12A], [12B], [13B], [22B], [35B], [37A].

13. A number of statistics where there is known to be a considerable degree of inequality (premature death, young adult suicides) have been trending downward steadily. [35A], [22A]

Educational outcomes at the bottom

There are two aspects of children's educational outcomes that are of interest from the point of view of deprivation. The first is how well children from deprived backgrounds do compared with children from non-deprived ones. Here the concern is with the strength of the link between childhood disadvantage and educational outcomes.

The second is the number of children who fail to reach some minimum educational standard. The concern here is that those with few or no qualifications are at greater risk of poverty in adult life than those with better qualifications. The evidence for this concern presented here is the finding that the lower a person's level of qualifications, the higher are the risks either of being out of, but wanting, work or being in work but low paid. [20B, 21B]

Continuing improvements at primary school level

At primary level, the evidence suggests there has been a steady and sustained improvement in both aspects of interest. The standard for comparison is level 4 in the Key Stage 2 tests taken by all children in the last year of primary school. Since level 4 is defined as the target level for this age group, it is reasonable to see this as a 'minimum' standard. Over the last decade, the proportion of children failing to reach that standard in England has fallen from 43 per cent to 21 per cent for English, and from 46 per cent to 25 per cent in Maths. Over the same period, the proportions have also fallen for schools containing a high number of children from deprived backgrounds, from above 60 per cent to around 35 per cent for both English and Maths. [14A] In other words, though the proportions for schools with more deprived children are around a third higher, they have come down in line with the average.

As a measure of how well deprived *children* do, outcomes for deprived *schools* are a proxy only. Direct information on how deprived children themselves do is now available, although it is too soon to draw any conclusions about trends. In 2005, however, children from deprived backgrounds were around twice as likely to fall short of level 4 at Key Stage 2 as children from non-deprived backgrounds (40 per cent compared with 20 per cent for English and 45 per cent compared to 25 per cent for Maths). This pattern holds for all ethnic groups, but is most pronounced for white children. In particular, while the 20 per cent of *non-deprived* white children failing to achieve level 4 is much less than the equivalent proportion for most minority ethnic groups, the 45 per cent of *deprived* white children failing to achieve level 4 is similar to that for most minority ethnic groups. In other words, deprived white children are equally likely to fail to achieve level 4 as deprived children from ethnic minorities. [14B]

Stagnation at secondary level and beyond

In contrast with the improvement at age 11, the story at age 16 and beyond is one of stagnation from around the start of the decade onwards, following an earlier period of slight improvement. Wider awareness of this is clouded by the fact that on the headline measure at age 16, that is, those achieving at least five GCSEs at grades C or above, the proportion failing to reach that level in England and Wales has declined steadily from 57 per cent in 1994/95 to 42 per cent in 2005/06. [15A]

It would be hard to characterise five GCSEs at grade C or above in the same way as level 4 at Key Stage 2 for 11-year-olds, that is, as something that all children ought to achieve. It was, after all, only in 2001/02 when a majority of 16-year-olds first reached that standard. By contrast, five GCSEs at *any* grade is a level that the vast majority of 16-year-olds have reached for a long time. This therefore seems a better candidate for a minimum standard at 16 than five GCSEs at grade C or above.

In the mid-1990s, 14 per cent of 16-year-olds failed to reach that level. By 1999/00, that proportion had dropped to 11 per cent, which is where it has remained ever since. [15A]

This picture of stagnation since around the start of the decade can also be seen in the levels of attainment for 19-year-olds: 27 per cent of 19-year-olds in 2005/06 lack qualifications to NVQ2 or equivalent.

Yet another statistic, in this case the proportion of 16-year-olds not in education or training (including a job which itself includes no training), shows a similar pattern, namely progress during the second half of the 1990s coming to a halt around the turn of the decade. [18A] Somewhat disturbingly, it also appears that these statistics on teenagers not in education or training are now no longer being collected in England.

The vast majority of those who achieve five GCSEs at age 16 go on to achieve further academic or vocational qualifications. By contrast, two-thirds of those who fail to achieve this standard at age 16 do not achieve it (or its vocational equivalent, NVQ2) by age 25. Furthermore, the one-third who do make further progress appear to achieve it by age 19. In other words, failure to reach that level by 16, whilst important, is not decisive but it does become decisive if not rectified in the two or three years immediately afterwards. [17B]

As with the equivalent information for primary schools, direct information on how deprived children do compared with non-deprived children has only recently (2004) become publicly available so it is too soon to draw any conclusions about trends. It is also only publicly available for the higher threshold of five or more GCSEs at grades C or above. In 2005, 70 per cent of deprived 16-year-olds failed to achieve this standard compared to 45 per cent of non-deprived 16-year-olds. But again what stands out is the much greater differences for white 16-year-olds with or without free school meals than for those from minority ethnic groups. Indeed, the proportion of deprived white 16-year-olds who do not achieve five or more GCSEs at grade C or above is higher than for any of the main minority ethnic groups. [15B] It is also noticeable that the proportion of white 16-year-olds no longer in full-time education is higher than for any ethnic minority. [18B]

The stagnation in outcomes for children with the lowest level of education attainment at ages 16 and 19 is quite at odds with outcomes at both younger ages and at other levels. While it makes no difference to poverty today, substantial and sustained reductions in poverty in the long term depend on raising the level of qualifications among older teenagers and young adults in the bottom quarter of educational achievement. The absence of progress here is a major concern for longer term progress on poverty reduction.

Summary of key points

14. Over the last decade, the proportion of 11-year-olds failing to reach level 4 at Key Stage 2 has continued to fall, from 43 per cent to 21 per cent for English, and from 46 per cent to 25 per cent in Maths. These proportions are also falling for schools with a high number of children from deprived backgrounds, from above 60 per cent to around 35 per cent for both English and Maths. [14A]

15. Despite continued progress in the proportion of 16-year-olds failing to reach the 'headline' level of five GCSEs at grade C or above (from 57 per cent in 1994/95 to 42 per cent in 2005/06), the proportion failing to get five GCSEs at any level has been stuck at 11 per cent since 1999/00. [15A]

16. The proportion of 19-year-olds who fail to reach the level of NVQ2 or equivalent is, at 27 per cent, the same as in 1996/97 and slightly higher than 2001/02. The proportion of 16-year-olds not in education or training has remained unchanged at 15 per cent since 2000. [17A], [18A]

17. At both 11 and 16, deprived white children are as likely to fail to reach educational thresholds as deprived children from ethnic minorities. [14B] [15B]

Exclusion by institutions

Government-backed successes

Two examples where there has been considerable recent success in reducing exclusion is lack of a bank account and lack of central heating, a common factor between these being that government has chosen to make an issue of them.

The problem of financial exclusion was addressed during the government's first term of office. The concern here was that households without a bank account were disadvantaged in various ways (for example through higher gas, electricity and water charges as a result of their being unable to pay by cheque or direct debit). The issue was that poor households were much more likely than households with average incomes to be without an account. By 2004/05, the proportion of households in the poorest fifth without a bank account had fallen to 10 per cent, compared with over 20 per cent in the late 1990s. [44A] Although no legislative action was taken, it is plausible to view this sharp fall as an industry-led response to concerns that were shared by government.

Central heating, as part of the wider issues of energy efficiency and fuel poverty, has been a government concern for a number of years, with a number of policy initiatives to improve matters. The concern has been with both the overall numbers without central heating, and the fact that the poorest households were more likely to lack it than others. Since at least the mid 1990s, both the overall proportion and the (previously) higher likelihood that poor households will suffer from the problem have come down steadily, to below 10 per cent in both cases in 2003/04. Indeed the proportion of poor households who lacked central heating in 2003/04 was actually less than that for households on average incomes just five years earlier. [48A]

Failures in public, private and voluntary sectors

Some examples of institutional behaviour that worsens poverty can be traced directly to central and local government. The proportion of households who are in poverty yet pay full Council Tax has risen from around 45 per cent in the late 1990s to 58 per cent in 2004/05. [25A] For these households, Council Tax either tips them over the line into poverty or pushes them further beneath it. One consequence of these figures (which are for England and Wales) is that almost half of all children in poverty (1.5 million) live in households paying full Council Tax. [25B]

Part of the problem here is non take-up of Council Tax Benefit by households who are entitled to it. This problem is particularly acute for pensioners, where the estimated proportion of entitled household who are not claiming the benefit has risen from under 30 per cent in 1997/98 to over 40 per cent in 2003/04. Over the same period there have been similar rises in the proportion of pensioner households not claiming Pension Credit (from under 30 per cent to nearly 40 per cent) and Housing Benefit (10 per cent to 15 per cent). [39A] Non-take-up of benefits is a problem of administration. The high number of households in poverty paying full Council Tax is also a problem of design, the Council Tax Benefit rules requiring households in work to start paying the tax even when their income is too low for Income Tax.

Another example of the way in which government may have exacerbated exclusion is the fall in the proportion of older people provided with help to live at home by their local authority, down (across England) by more than a third in 10 years. At the same time as the total number helped has come down, the proportion provided with intensive help has gone up. [42A] Any overall conclusion about whether exclusion has been improved or worsened here requires a judgement about how to compare these two types of help. That there are choices about how much help to provide is made plain by the fact the proportions helped differ substantially according to the type of local authority, with county councils helping only two-thirds as many as Inner London and Welsh authorities. [42B]

Although banks and building societies may claim credit for reducing the number of poor households without bank accounts, there are other financial products where the gap in provision between poor and average households is still large. One example is home contents insurance, lacked by just 20 per cent of households on average incomes compared with 50 per cent of households in the poorest fifth. [45B]

Households without cars are twice as likely as households with cars to report difficulties in accessing essential local services such as shops, supermarkets, doctors, post offices and hospitals. [46A] It is clearly not possible to hold any one institution responsible for problems to do with the accessibility of services. It is, however, clear that two of the groups most affected by these problems are single pensioners and lone parent families, these being the households most likely to lack a car. [46B]

All of these examples of institutional exclusion apply to people as consumers or clients. But there are also examples that apply to people as employees or would-be employees. The first concerns people with a work-limiting disability who want to work. The key point here, which has already been discussed, is that the negative effect of such disabilities on the likelihood of being in work are greater than the positive effects of better qualifications. In particular, at every level of qualification, from higher education level to no more than GCSEs at a low grade, the proportion of people with a work-limiting disability who want but lack work is at least three times the rate for similarly qualified people without a disability. [28B] This does not mean that the cause of the problem is active or deliberate discrimination on the part of employers. But, whatever the cause, it does show that disabled people suffer substantial exclusion from employment as a result of the way that the labour market works.

Labour market exclusion is not just about getting into work but also about what happens once there. One example of this is workplace training: whilst there has been some improvement since 1998, people without qualifications are still only a third as likely to have received training recently than people with qualifications. [34A]

Finally, there is the question of whether trade unions are representing low paid workers as well as better paid ones. The evidence here suggests they are not, with just 13 per cent of workers earning less than £6.50 an hour being a member of a union, half the rate for those earning £21 an hour or more and one third the rate for those earning £15 to £21. [34B]

Summary of key points

18. The proportion of low income households without a bank account fell to 10 per cent by 2004/05, down from well above 20 per cent in the late 1990s. The proportion of low income households without central heating has, coincidentally, fallen at an equally rapid rate. In both cases, the gap between low income households and households on average incomes is now small. [44A], [48A]

19. The proportion of households in poverty paying full Council Tax has gone up steadily, from 45 per cent in 1998/99 to 58 per cent in 2004/05. 1.5 million children in poverty live in households paying full Council Tax. [25A], [25B]

20. At every level of qualification, the proportion of people with a work-limiting disability who want but lack work is at least three times the rate for similarly qualified people without a disability. [28B]

21. In 2005, 13 per cent of employees earning £6.50 an hour or less belonged to a trade union, compared with 43 per cent for those earnings between £15 and £21 an hour, and 28 per cent for those earning £21 an hour and above. [34B]

Notes

1 Throughout this discussion, where evidence is sourced from the graphs, it is referred to by its indicator number and 'A' or 'B' to indicate whether it is the first or second of the pair.

2 Hirsch J. *What will it take to end child poverty? Firing on all cylinders*. York: Joseph Rowntree Foundation, 2006.

3 On a technical point, we are using the word 'family' here to describe what are referred to as 'benefit units' in the *Households Below Average Income* dataset. In this official terminology, a 'household' (which more or less has its ordinary meaning) can contain more than one 'benefit unit': and indeed there are about one third more 'benefit units' than 'households' in this particular dataset.

4 The source for the quoted statistic is the Labour Force Survey.

5 For a fuller analysis of this issue, see Winckler V. and Kenway P. *A scoping study on in-work poverty in Wales*. The Bevan Institute, 2006. Available at www.npi.org.uk.

6 The low pay threshold used here is one that rises in line with average earnings and reaches £6.50 in 2005. It is therefore £4.81 in 1998, £5.02 in 1999, £5.30 in 2000, £5.55 in 2001, £5.71 in 2002, £5.91 in 2003, £6.22 in 2004 and £6.50 in 2005.

7 In this case, a low paid woman is one whose earnings are one tenth of the way up the scale of all female earnings while a low paid man is the one whose earnings are one tenth of the way up the scale of all male earnings. In order to aid comparability, the earnings of both are expressed in relation to *male* median earnings, that is, the earnings of the man exactly half way up the scale of all male earnings.

8 For example, see Brewer N., Goodman A., Shaw J., and Sibieta L. *Poverty and inequality in Britain: 2006*. London: The Institute of Fiscal Studies, 2006.

Chapter 1
Low income

Indicators

Trends in low income

1 **Numbers in low income**

2 **The impact of housing costs**

3 **Low income by age group**

4 **Income inequalities**

5 **Lacking essential items**

In receipt of state benefits

6 **Out-of-work benefit levels**

7 **Long-term working-age recipients of out-of-work benefits**

Low income

This chapter has two themes containing seven indicators in total. The themes are:

■ trends in low income;

■ in receipt of state benefits.

Trends in low income

Choice of indicators

This theme provides a range of information on both the number and proportion of people with low income in terms of both trends and groups.

The principal measure of low income is a household income that is 60 per cent or less of the contemporary average (median) household income after deducting housing costs. In the most recent year, 2004/05, that threshold, adjusted for the number of people living in the household, was worth:

■ £100 a week for a single adult;

■ £183 a week for a two adult household;

■ £186 a week for a single adult living with two children;

■ £268 a week for two adults living with two children.

This sum of money is after income tax and national insurance have been deducted from earnings and after council tax, rent, mortgage and water charges have been paid. It is therefore what a household has available to spend on everything else it needs.

In recognition that the government is in the process of adopting a more complex approach to the measurement of poverty, the theme also presents some information on lack of essential items as well as low income before deducting housing costs.

The first graph of the first indicator shows how the number of people living in low income households has changed over time. As well as the principal measure of 60 per cent of contemporary average household income after deducting housing costs (a threshold which rises as the country becomes richer), it also shows the number of people living below a fixed income threshold, namely 60 per cent of average household income in 1996/97 (after adjusting for price inflation). The supporting graph shows how the proportion of people in low income households in the United Kingdom compares with that in the other pre-accession countries of the European Union.

The second indicator shows how the number of people in low income households after deducting housing costs compares with the number before deducting housing costs. This is done in recognition of the government's apparent plans to adopt the before deducting housing cost measure for its future poverty targets. The first graph shows the differences over time and the second graph shows the differences by region.

The third indicator provides an analysis by age group. The first graph shows the risk of a person being in a low income household, with the data shown separately for children, pensioners and working-age adults. The supporting graph provides a breakdown of the people in low income households by age group.

The fourth indicator is concerned with income inequalities. For each tenth of the population, the first graph shows the change in the real incomes over the last decade in terms of both the percentages and absolute numbers. The supporting graph shows how the proportions of people in the poorest and richest fifths of the population vary by region.

The final indicator looks at the proportion of households who 'do not have because they cannot afford' particular kinds of essential items and activities. The first graph provides an analysis of the 2004/05 Family Resources Survey, when questions of this type were first asked. The second graph provides an analysis of more comprehensive, but older, data dating from 1999.

What the indicators show

Indicator 1 Numbers in low income

The number of people in relative low income is now lower than at any time since 1987, but it is still much higher than in the early 1980s.

The UK has a higher proportion of its population on relative low income than nine other pre-accession EU countries but a lower proportion than five.

Indicator 2 The impact of housing costs

The numbers of people in low income is lower on a 'before deducting housing costs' measure than on an 'after deducting housing costs' measure, although the gap has narrowed over the last decade.

The proportion of people in low income in Southern England is much higher on an 'after deducting housing costs' measure than on a 'before deducting housing costs' measure.

Indicator 3 Low income by age group

The proportion of children and pensioners who live in low income households has been falling. By contrast, the proportion for working-age adults without dependent children has remained broadly unchanged.

A third of all people in low income households are working-age adults without dependent children.

Indicator 4 Income inequalities

Over the last decade, the richest tenth of the population have seen their income increase the most and the poorest tenth have seen their incomes increase the least.

Inner London is deeply divided: it has by far the highest proportion of people on a low income but also a high proportion of people on a high income.

Indicator 5 Lacking essential items

Many people on low incomes say that they cannot afford selected essential items – but so do quite a lot of people on average incomes.

The essential items that are most commonly lacking are those which are directly money-related.

In receipt of state benefits

Choice of indicators

This theme provides information on both the number of recipients of out-of-work benefits and the value of the benefits that they receive.

The first graph of the first indicator shows how the value of Income Support has varied over time for selected family types. The supporting graph provides a breakdown of out-of-work benefit recipients by family type.

The second indicator shows how the number of working-age people in receipt of out-of-work benefit for two years or more has changed over time, with the data broken down by type of claimant. The majority of long-term claimants of out-of-work benefits are sick or disabled and, in this context, the supporting graph provides an age breakdown of those who have either been in receipt of Incapacity Benefit for two years or more or are in receipt of Severe Disablement Allowance.

What the indicators show

Indicator 6 Out-of-work benefit levels

While the level of Income Support for both pensioners and families with two or more children is higher, relative to earnings, than it was in the late 1990s, the level for working-age adults without children is much lower.

Almost half of all adults reliant on state benefits are of working age and do not have dependent children.

Indicator 7 Long-term working-age recipients of out-of-work benefits

Three-quarters of working-age people receiving a key out-of-work benefit for two years or more are sick or disabled.

Two-thirds of the long-term claimants of Incapacity Benefit or Severe Disablement Allowance are aged less than 55 and a third are aged less than 45.

Numbers in low income

1A: The number of people in relative low income is now lower than at any time since 1987, but it is still much higher than in the early 1980s.

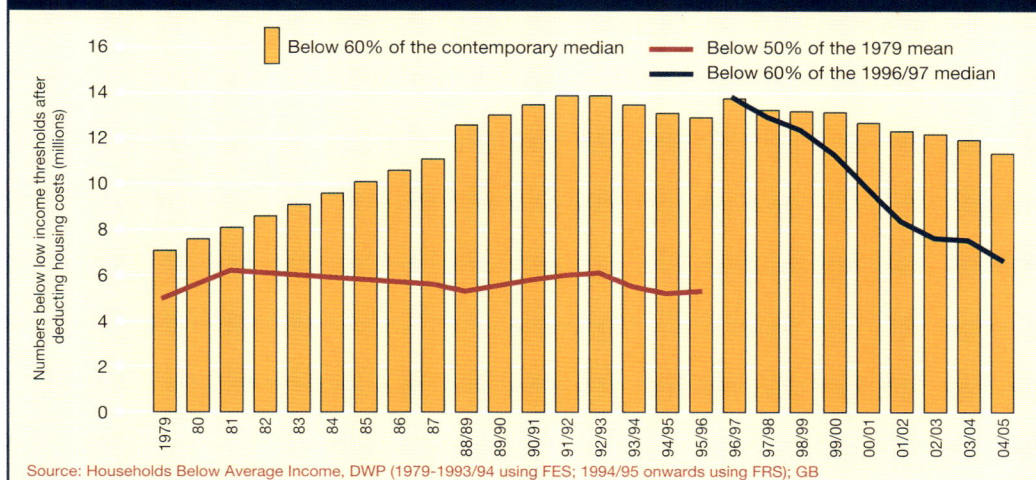

Legend: Below 60% of the contemporary median — Below 50% of the 1979 mean — Below 60% of the 1996/97 median

Y-axis: Numbers below low income thresholds after deducting housing costs (millions)

Source: Households Below Average Income, DWP (1979-1993/94 using FES; 1994/95 onwards using FRS); GB

1B: The UK has a higher proportion of its population on relative low income than nine other pre-accession EU countries but a lower proportion than five.

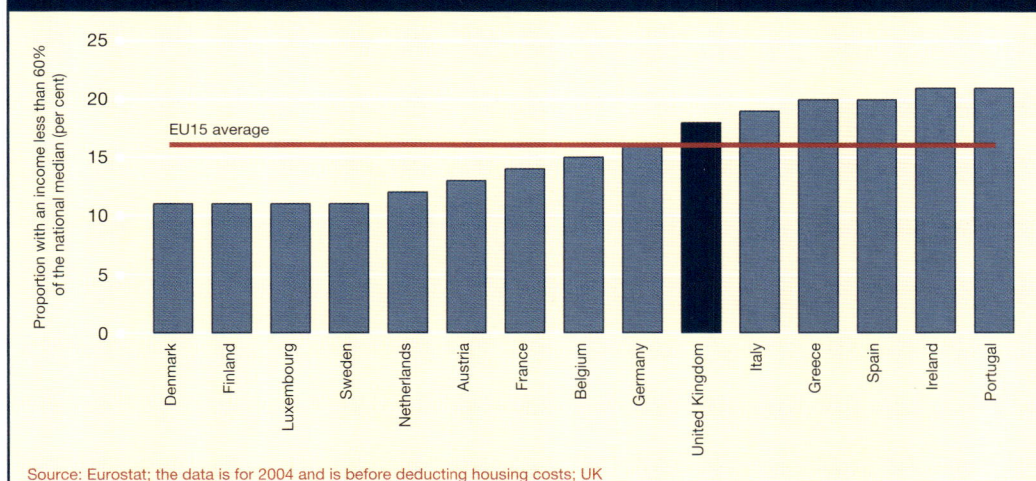

Y-axis: Proportion with an income less than 60% of the national median (per cent)

EU15 average

Countries: Denmark, Finland, Luxembourg, Sweden, Netherlands, Austria, France, Belgium, Germany, United Kingdom, Italy, Greece, Spain, Ireland, Portugal

Source: Eurostat; the data is for 2004 and is before deducting housing costs; UK

The bars in the first graph show the number of people in households below 60 per cent of contemporary median income for each year since 1979. The line from 1996/97 onwards shows the number of people below a fixed threshold of 60 per cent of 1996/97 median income (adjusted for price inflation). The line from 1979 to 1994/95 shows the number of people below a fixed threshold of 50 per cent of 1979 mean income (adjusted for price inflation) – 50 per cent of mean being the threshold of low income commonly used at the time. The data source is Households Below Average Income, based on the Family Resources Survey (FRS) since 1994/95 and the Family Expenditure Survey (FES) for earlier years. The data relates to Great Britain. Income is disposable household income after deducting housing costs. All data is equivalised (adjusted) to account for variation in household size and composition. The self-employed are included in the statistics.

The second graph shows the proportions of people in EU countries with an equivalised household income that was less than 60 per cent of the median for their country. The EU average shown is the average weighted by population. The data source is the European Community Household Panel Survey and is for 2004. Note that this data is not comparable with the income poverty statistics in the other graphs.

Overall adequacy of the indicator: high. The FRS and FES are both well-established annual government surveys, designed to be representative of the population as a whole.

The Impact of housing costs

2A: The numbers of people in low income is lower on a 'before deducting housing costs' measure than on an 'after deducting housing costs' measure, although the gap has narrowed over the last decade.

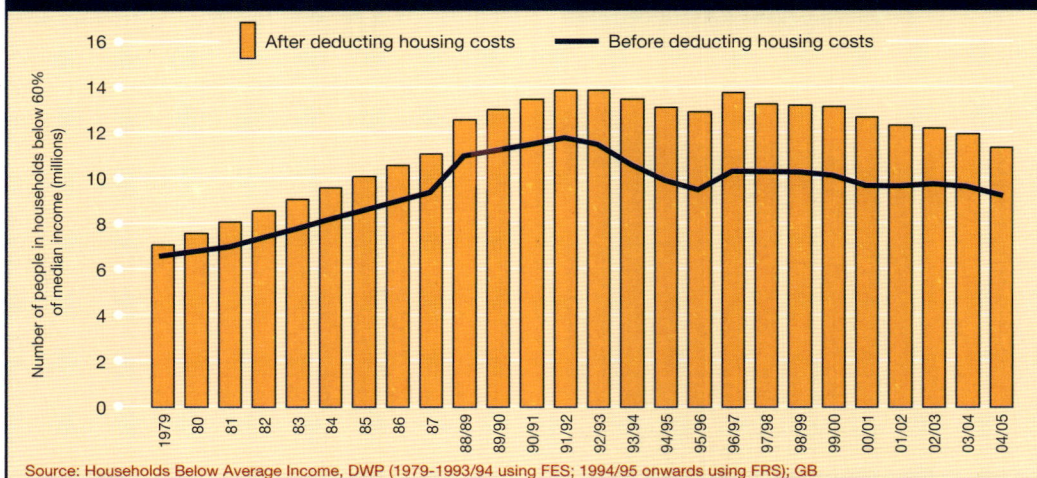

Legend: After deducting housing costs | Before deducting housing costs

Y-axis: Number of people in households below 60% of median income (millions)

X-axis: 1979, 80, 81, 82, 83, 84, 85, 86, 87, 88/89, 89/90, 90/91, 91/92, 92/93, 93/94, 94/95, 95/96, 96/97, 97/98, 98/99, 99/00, 00/01, 01/02, 02/03, 03/04, 04/05

Source: Households Below Average Income, DWP (1979-1993/94 using FES; 1994/95 onwards using FRS); GB

2B: The proportion of people in low income in Southern England is much higher on an 'after deducting housing costs' measure than on a 'before deducting housing costs' measure.

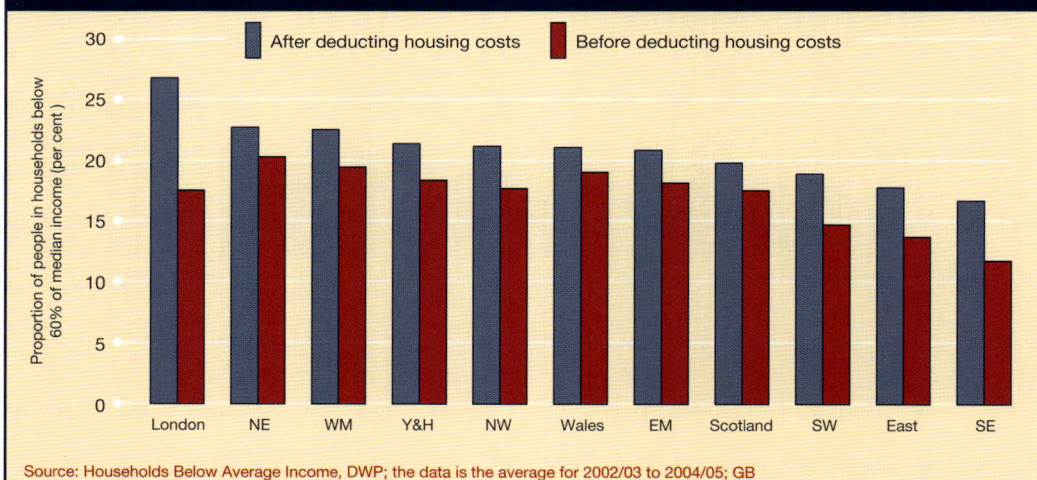

Legend: After deducting housing costs | Before deducting housing costs

Y-axis: Proportion of people in households below 60% of median income (per cent)

X-axis: London, NE, WM, Y&H, NW, Wales, EM, Scotland, SW, East, SE

Source: Households Below Average Income, DWP; the data is the average for 2002/03 to 2004/05; GB

The first graph shows the number of people in households below 60 per cent of contemporary median income for each year since 1979, both before and after deducting housing costs.

The second graph shows how the proportion of people who are in households below 60 per cent of contemporary median income varies by region, again both before and after deducting housing costs. To improve its statistical reliability, the data is the average for the latest three years.

The data source for both graphs is Households Below Average Income, based on the Family Resources Survey (FRS) since 1994/95 and the Family Expenditure Survey (FES) for earlier years. The data relates to Great Britain. Income is disposable household income. All data is equivalised (adjusted) to account for variation in household size and composition. The self-employed are included in the statistics.

Overall adequacy of the indicator: high. The FRS and FES are both well-established annual government surveys, designed to be representative of the population as a whole.

Low income by age group

3A: The proportion of children and pensioners who live in low income households has been falling. By contrast, the proportion for working-age adults without dependent children has remained broadly unchanged.

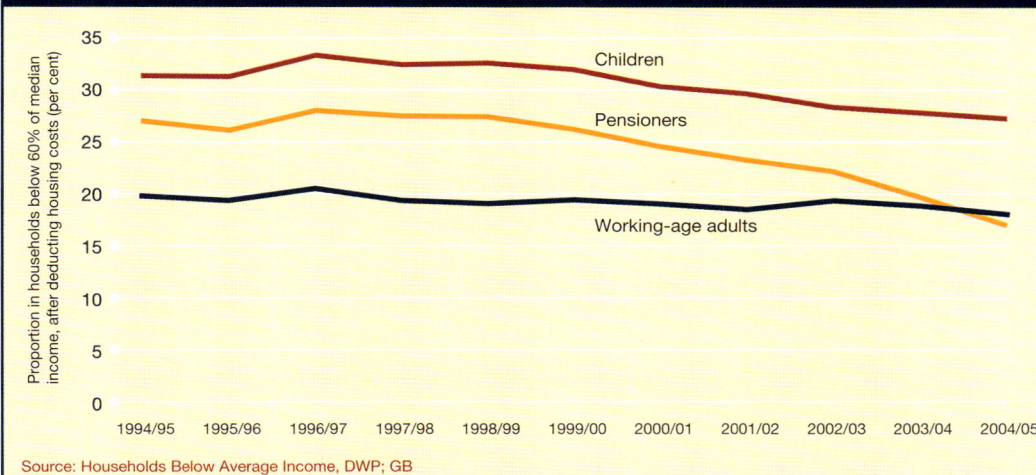

Proportion in households below 60% of median income, after deducting housing costs (per cent)

- Children
- Pensioners
- Working-age adults

1994/95 1995/96 1996/97 1997/98 1998/99 1999/00 2000/01 2001/02 2002/03 2003/04 2004/05

Source: Households Below Average Income, DWP; GB

3B: A third of all people in low income households are working-age adults without dependent children.

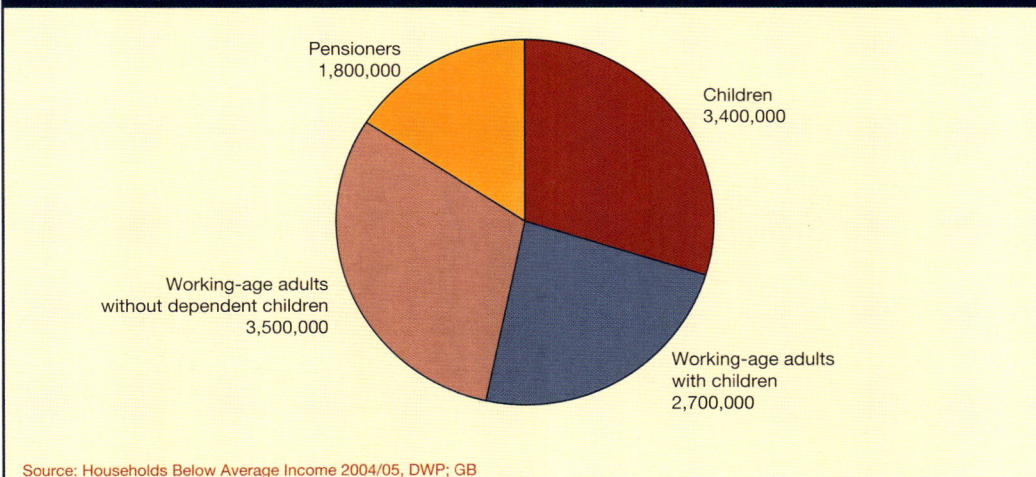

Pensioners 1,800,000

Children 3,400,000

Working-age adults without dependent children 3,500,000

Working-age adults with children 2,700,000

Source: Households Below Average Income 2004/05, DWP; GB

The first graph shows the risk of a person being in a low income household, with the data shown separately for children, pensioners and working-age adults.

The second graph shows, for the latest year, a breakdown of the people in low income households according to whether they are children, pensioners, working-age adults with dependent children or working-age adults without dependent children.

The data source for both graphs is Households Below Average Income, based on the Family Resources Survey (FRS). The data relates to Great Britain. The self-employed are included in the statistics. Income is disposable household income after deducting housing costs. All data is equivalised (adjusted) to account for variation in household size and composition.

Overall adequacy of the indicator: high. The FRS is a well-established annual government survey, designed to be representative of the population as a whole.

Income inequalities

4A: Over the last decade, the richest tenth of the population have seen their income increase the most and the poorest tenth have seen their incomes increase the least.

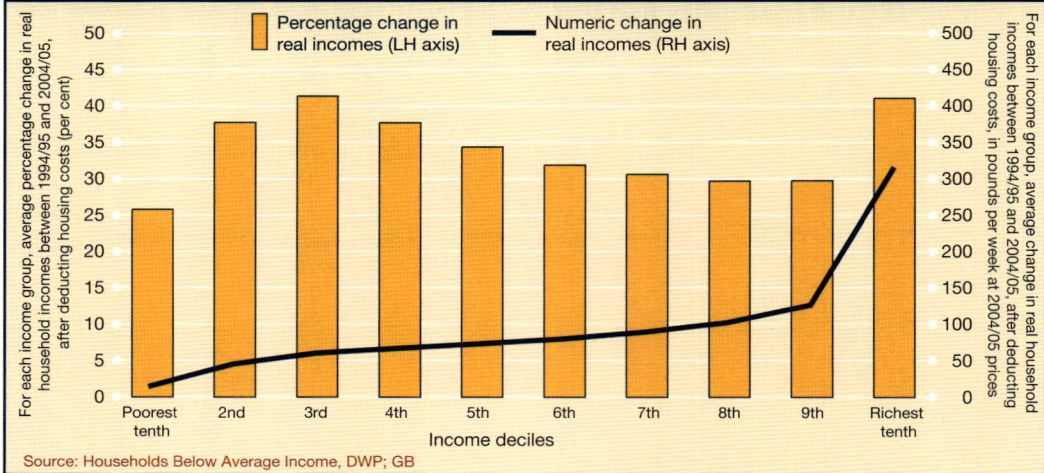

For each income group, average percentage change in real household incomes between 1994/95 and 2004/05, after deducting housing costs (per cent)

Legend:
- Percentage change in real incomes (LH axis)
- Numeric change in real incomes (RH axis)

Income deciles: Poorest tenth, 2nd, 3rd, 4th, 5th, 6th, 7th, 8th, 9th, Richest tenth

For each income group, average change in real household incomes between 1994/95 and 2004/05, after deducting housing costs, in pounds per week at 2004/05 prices

Source: Households Below Average Income, DWP; GB

4B: Inner London is deeply divided: it has by far the highest proportion of people on a low income but also a high proportion of people on a high income.

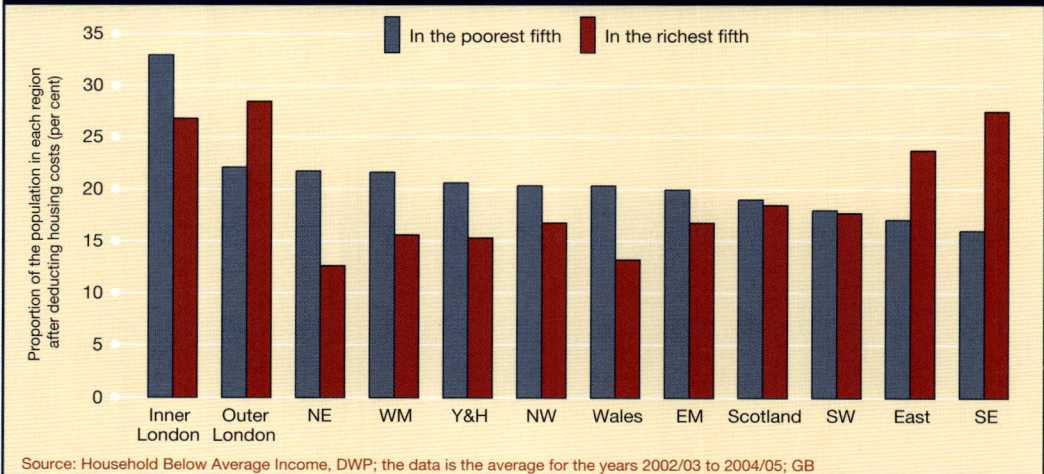

Proportion of the population in each region after deducting housing costs (per cent)

Legend:
- In the poorest fifth
- In the richest fifth

Regions: Inner London, Outer London, NE, WM, Y&H, NW, Wales, EM, Scotland, SW, East, SE

Source: Household Below Average Income, DWP; the data is the average for the years 2002/03 to 2004/05; GB

The first graph shows the average change in real incomes for each income decile over the decade to 2004/05. The bars show the change as a proportion of 1994/95 income (after adjusting for inflation) whilst the line shows the change in terms of absolute amounts in pounds per week (using 2004/05 prices).

The second graph shows the proportion of the population whose income is in the lowest and highest income quintiles (fifths) in each region in Great Britain. Inner and Outer London are presented separately as the results are so different. To improve its statistical reliability, the data is the average for the latest three years.

The data source for both graphs is Households Below Average Income, based on the Family Resources Survey (FRS). Income is disposable household income after housing costs. All data is equivalised (adjusted) to account for variation in household size and composition. The self-employed are included in the statistics.

Overall adequacy of the indicator: high. The FRS is a well-established annual government survey, designed to be representative of the population as a whole.

Lacking essential items

5A: Many people on low incomes say that they cannot afford selected essential items – but so do quite a lot of people on average incomes.

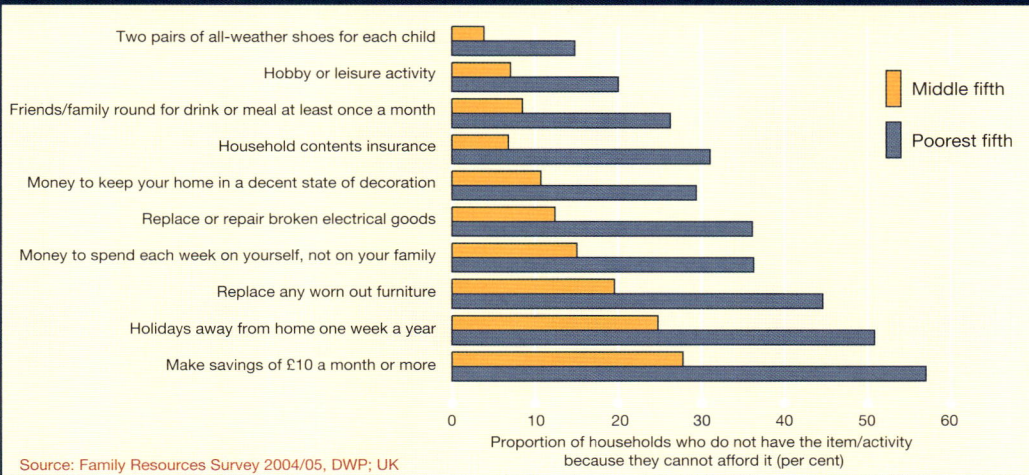

Two pairs of all-weather shoes for each child
Hobby or leisure activity
Friends/family round for drink or meal at least once a month
Household contents insurance
Money to keep your home in a decent state of decoration
Replace or repair broken electrical goods
Money to spend each week on yourself, not on your family
Replace any worn out furniture
Holidays away from home one week a year
Make savings of £10 a month or more

Middle fifth
Poorest fifth

0   10   20   30   40   50   60

Proportion of households who do not have the item/activity
because they cannot afford it (per cent)

Source: Family Resources Survey 2004/05, DWP; UK

5B: The essential items that are mostly commonly lacking are those which are directly money-related.

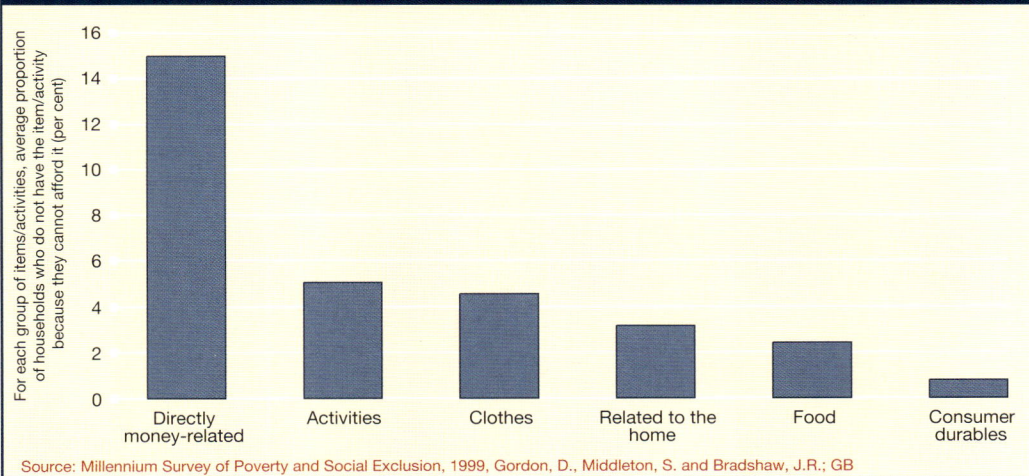

For each group of items/activities, average proportion of households who do not have the item/activity because they cannot afford it (per cent)

16
14
12
10
8
6
4
2
0

Directly money-related   Activities   Clothes   Related to the home   Food   Consumer durables

Source: Millennium Survey of Poverty and Social Exclusion, 1999, Gordon, D., Middleton, S. and Bradshaw, J.R.; GB

The graphs in this indicator look at the proportion of households who 'do not have because they cannot afford' particular kinds of essential items and activities. The first graph provides an analysis of the 2004/05 Family Resources Survey, when question of this type were first asked. For each of a selected number of items/activities, it shows the proportion of households who 'do not have it because they cannot afford it', with the data shown separately for households in the poorest fifth and for households on average incomes. The data relates to the United Kingdom. Household income is disposable household income after deducting housing costs, where the income has been equivalised (adjusted) to account for variation in household size and composition.

The second graph provides an analysis of a one-off survey called *Millennium Survey of Poverty and Social Exclusion 1999*, which asked questions about 35 essential items/activities. It arranges these into six groups, namely money-related, clothes, activities, related to the home, food and consumer durables and, for each group, shows the average proportion of households who 'do not have because they cannot afford' an item/activity in the group. The data relates to Great Britain.

Overall adequacy of the indicator: limited. The data is subjective and, as illustrated in the first graph, many households with average incomes nevertheless say that they cannot afford essential items/activities.

Out-of-work benefit levels

6A: While the level of Income Support for both pensioners and families with two or more children is higher, relative to earnings, than it was in the late 1990s, the level for working-age adults without children is much lower.

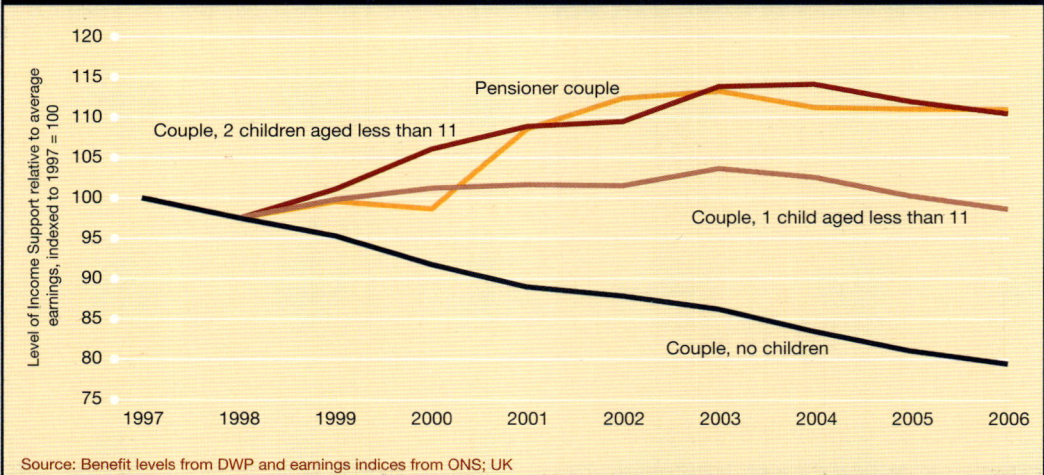

Level of Income Support relative to average earnings, indexed to 1997 = 100

Pensioner couple

Couple, 2 children aged less than 11

Couple, 1 child aged less than 11

Couple, no children

Source: Benefit levels from DWP and earnings indices from ONS; UK

6B: Almost half of all adults reliant on state benefits are of working age and do not have dependent children.

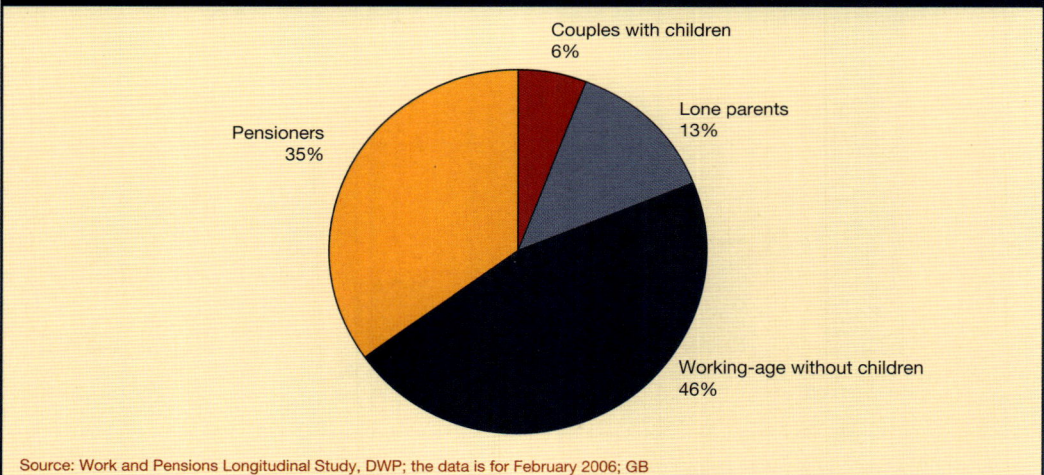

Couples with children 6%

Lone parents 13%

Pensioners 35%

Working-age without children 46%

Source: Work and Pensions Longitudinal Study, DWP; the data is for February 2006; GB

The first graph show how the value of Income Support has varied over time for pensioner couples, couples with two children aged less than 11, couples with 1 child aged less than 11 and couples with no children. In each case, the base year is 1997, at which point the value of the benefits is set to 100. The subsequent figures are deflated by the growth in average earnings using the seasonally adjusted figures from the ONS Average Earnings Index. The family types were selected to best illustrate the differing trends over time. So, for example, single adults with no dependent children is not shown as it has followed similar trends to that for couples with no dependent children. No disability benefits have been included.

The second graph provides a breakdown of the recipients of one or more 'key out-of-work benefits'. 'Key out-of-work benefits' is a Department for Work and Pensions (DWP) term which covers the following benefits: Jobseeker's Allowance, Income Support, Incapacity Benefit, Severe Disablement Allowance, Carer's Allowance and Pension Credit. The data source is the DWP Work and Pensions Longitudinal Study. The data has been analysed to avoid double-counting of those receiving multiple benefits. The data relates to Great Britain and is for February 2006.

Overall adequacy of the indicator: high. The statistics in the first graph are factual.

Long-term working-age recipients of out-of-work benefits

7A: Three-quarters of working-age people receiving a key out-of-work benefit for two years or more are sick or disabled.

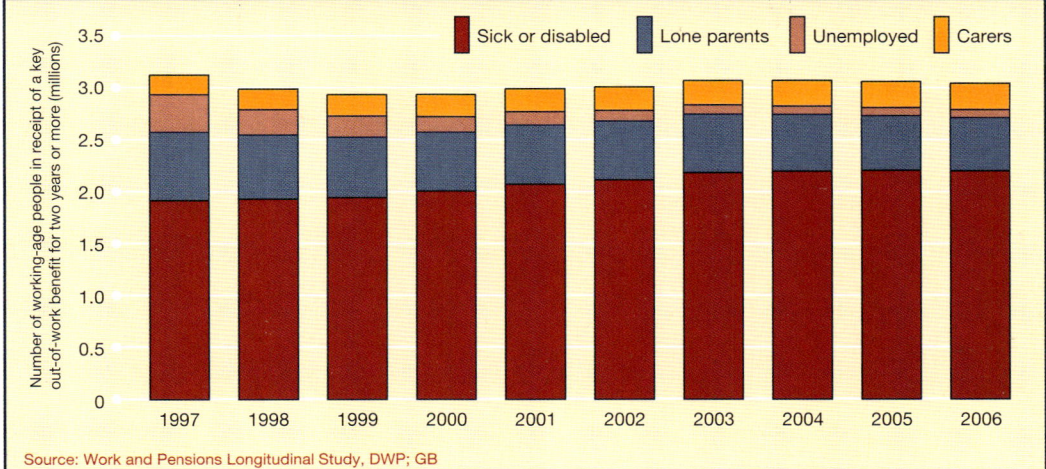

Legend: Sick or disabled — Lone parents — Unemployed — Carers

Y-axis: Number of working-age people in receipt of a key out-of-work benefit for two years or more (millions)

Source: Work and Pensions Longitudinal Study, DWP; GB

7B: Two-thirds of the long-term claimants of Incapacity Benefit or Severe Disablement Allowance are aged less than 55 and a third are aged less than 45.

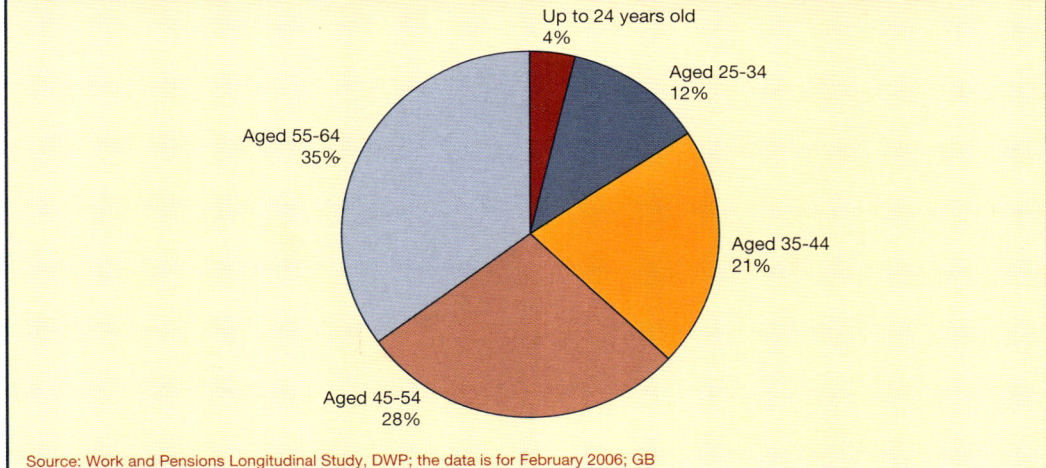

- Up to 24 years old 4%
- Aged 25-34 12%
- Aged 35-44 21%
- Aged 45-54 28%
- Aged 55-64 35%

Source: Work and Pensions Longitudinal Study, DWP; the data is for February 2006; GB

The first graph shows all those of working age who were in receipt of a 'key out-of-work benefit' for two years or more. 'Key out-of-work benefits' is a Department for Work and Pensions (DWP) term which covers the following benefits: Jobseeker's Allowance, Income Support, Incapacity Benefit, Severe Disablement Allowance and Carer's Allowance. For each year, the total is broken down by type of claimant, namely: unemployed, sick or disabled, lone parents and carers. Note that a small number of 'others' have been omitted from the graph.

As can be seen from the first graph, the majority of long-term claimants of key out-of-work benefits are sick or disabled. In this context, the second graph shows, for the latest year, an age breakdown for those who have either been in receipt of Incapacity Benefit for two years or more or are in receipt of Severe Disablement Allowance.

The data source for both graphs is the DWP Work and Pensions Longitudinal Study. The data relates to Great Britain and is for the month of February of each year. The data has been analysed to avoid double-counting of those receiving multiple benefits.

Overall adequacy of the indicator: high. The data is thought to be very reliable. It is based on information collected by the DWP for the administration of benefits.

Chapter 2
Children

Children

This chapter has three themes containing nine indicators in total. The themes are:

- economic circumstances;
- health and well-being;
- education.

Economic circumstances

Choice of indicators

The indicators provide three complementary views of child poverty in terms of both trends and groups.

The first indicator shows the trends in the number of children in low income households over the last decade, with the government's 2005 target and the figures for 1979 both also shown for comparison purposes. This information is provided both before and after deducting housing costs as the government's 2005 target was ambiguous about which it was using. The supporting graph shows the distribution of children in low income households according to the children's family type and work circumstances.

One of the key government initiatives to reduce child poverty has been the expansion of the tax credits system for working households. In this context, the second indicator provides an analysis of children according to both the tax credit status of their household and its level of income. The first graph shows the trends over time for three groups of children where, excluding tax credits (and their predecessors), the household is in low income. These groups are those not in receipt of tax credits, those in receipt of tax credits (over the above the family element) but still in low income, and those in receipt of tax credits where, as a result, they are no longer in low income. The second graph shows children who are in working households in receipt of tax credits, broken down by whether or not they remain in low income and whether or not they would have been in low income without the tax credits.

The final indicator shows how the number of children who are in workless households has changed over the last decade, with the data shown separately according to whether they are living with one parent or two. The supporting graph shows how the United Kingdom compared with the other countries of the European Union.

What the indicators show

Indicator 8 In low income households

The number of children in low income households has fallen steadily but not quickly enough to meet government targets.

Two-fifths of the children in low income households live in couple households where at least one of the adults is in paid work.

Indicator 9 In receipt of tax credits

Tax credits now take around 1 million children in working households out of low income – but 1¾ million still remain in low income.

Only a fifth of the children in households in receipt of tax credits are no longer in low income because of the tax credit monies received.

Indicator 10 In workless households

The number of children in workless households has fallen by a quarter over the last decade, with most of this fall being for children in couple households.

The UK has a higher proportion of its children living in workless households than any other EU country.

Health and well-being

Choice of indicators

These indicators covers a range of child health issues namely birthweight, infant death, dental health and underage pregnancy.

The first indicator covers low birthweight and shows trends over time by social class.

The first graph of the second indicator covers infant deaths and again shows trends over time by social class. The second graph of this indicator covers dental health and shows the differences in the number of decayed teeth by social class for 5- and 15-year-olds.

The final indicator covers underage pregnancy and shows trends over time separately for both births and abortions.

What the indicators show

Indicator 11 Low birthweight babies

Babies born to parents from manual social backgrounds continue to be more likely to have a low birthweight than those born to parents from non-manual social backgrounds.

Babies born to lone parents are more likely to be of low birthweight than babies born to couples.

Indicator 12 Child health

While the rate of infant death among those from non-manual social backgrounds has fallen over the last decade, the pattern for those from manual social backgrounds is less clear.

Children from routine and manual backgrounds have, on average, one more tooth with obvious tooth decay than other children.

Indicator 13 Underage pregnancies

While the number of births to girls conceiving under age 16 has fallen by a third since 1996, the number of abortions is unchanged.

Teenage motherhood is eight times as common amongst those from manual social backgrounds as for those from professional backgrounds.

Education

Choice of indicators

The first two indicators in this theme show the progress there has been over the last decade in the number of children reaching certain minimum educational standards. For 11-year-olds, the standard is level 4 at Key Stage 2 in each of Maths and English. For 16-year-olds, the standards are first, at least one GCSE and second, at least five GCSEs. The graph for the 11-year-olds also shows the results separately for schools containing a high proportion of children with low incomes, whilst the second also shows the trends for a higher threshold, namely at least five GCSEs at Grade C or above.

The supporting graphs take the comparison between poor children and other children further, showing the results separately by whether or not they get free school meals and their ethnic group. The GCSE standard being measured here is the higher one of at least five GCSEs at grade C or above.

The third indicator shows the trends in the number of children permanently excluded from school, with the supporting graph providing a further breakdown by ethnic group.

What the indicators show

Indicator 14 Low attainment at school (11-year-olds)

Progress continues to be made in the literacy and numeracy of 11-year-olds – including those in deprived schools.

Differences in achievement between 11-year-old pupils with/without free school meals are greatest amongst white pupils.

Indicator 15 Low attainment at school (16-year-olds)

12 per cent of 16-year-olds still obtain fewer than five GCSEs, the same as in 1998/99. This lack of improvement contrasts with the continuing improvement for the higher threshold of five GCSEs at grade C or above.

Three-quarters of white pupils in receipt of free school meals do not obtain five or more GCSEs at grade C or above.

Indicator 16 School exclusions

The number of permanent exclusions remained broadly unchanged over the last five years.

Despite substantial reductions in recent years, black Caribbean pupils are still three times as likely to be excluded from school as white pupils.

In low income households

8A: The number of children in low income households has fallen steadily but not quickly enough to meet government targets.

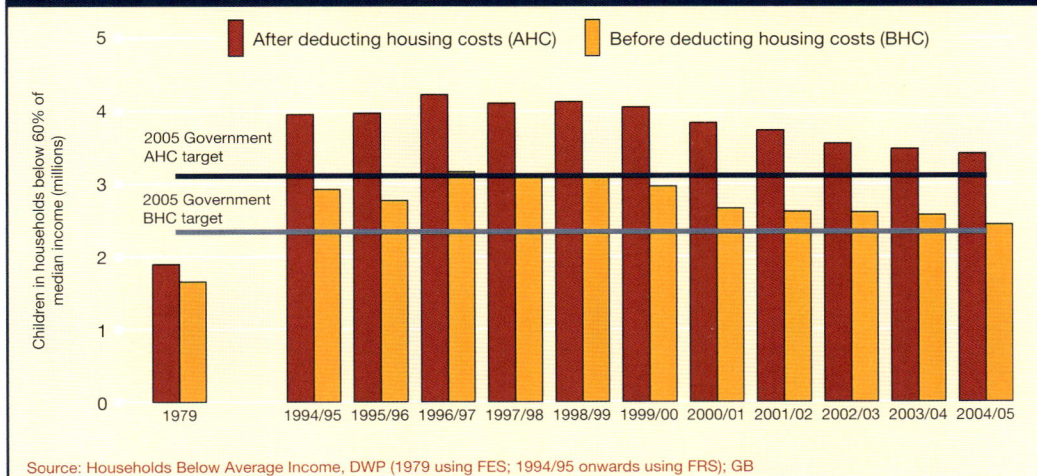

After deducting housing costs (AHC) **Before deducting housing costs (BHC)**

Children in households below 60% of median income (millions)

2005 Government AHC target

2005 Government BHC target

1979 1994/95 1995/96 1996/97 1997/98 1998/99 1999/00 2000/01 2001/02 2002/03 2003/04 2004/05

Source: Households Below Average Income, DWP (1979 using FES; 1994/95 onwards using FRS); GB

8B: Two-fifths of the children in low income households live in couple households where at least one of the adults is in paid work.

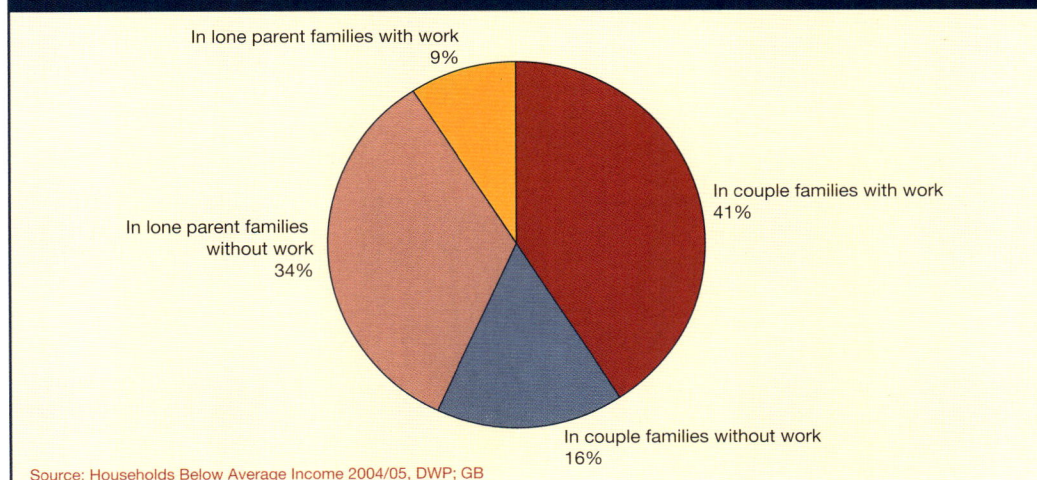

In lone parent families with work
9%

In couple families with work
41%

In lone parent families without work
34%

In couple families without work
16%

Source: Households Below Average Income 2004/05, DWP; GB

The first graph shows the number of children living in households below 60 per cent of median income, both before and after deducting housing costs. The graph also shows the government's target to reduce the number of children in poverty by a quarter by 2005 compared to the number in 1998/99, again both before and after deducting housing costs. The two measures are shown as the government's child poverty target for 2005 was ambiguous about which it was using.

The second graph shows, for the latest year, a breakdown of the children who were in low income households by family type (couple or lone parent) and work status (workless or someone in paid work).

The data source for both graphs is Households Below Average Income, based on the Family Resources Survey (FRS). The data relates to Great Britain. The self-employed are included in the statistics. Income is disposable household income and, in the second graph, is after deducting housing costs. All data is equivalised (adjusted) to account for variation in household size and composition.

Overall adequacy of the indicator: high. The FRS is a well-established annual government survey, designed to be representative of the population as a whole.

In receipt of tax credits

9A: Tax credits now take around 1 million children in working households out of low income – but 1¾ million still remain in low income.

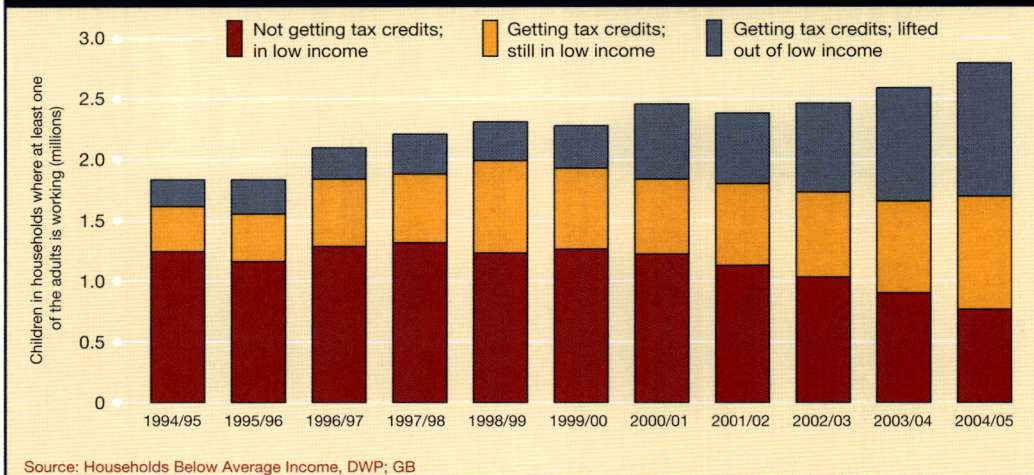

Legend:
- Not getting tax credits; in low income
- Getting tax credits; still in low income
- Getting tax credits; lifted out of low income

Y-axis: Children in households where at least one of the adults is working (millions), scale 0 to 3.0

X-axis years: 1994/95, 1995/96, 1996/97, 1997/98, 1998/99, 1999/00, 2000/01, 2001/02, 2002/03, 2003/04, 2004/05

Source: Households Below Average Income, DWP; GB

9B: Only a fifth of the children in households in receipt of tax credits are no longer in low income because of the tax credit monies received.

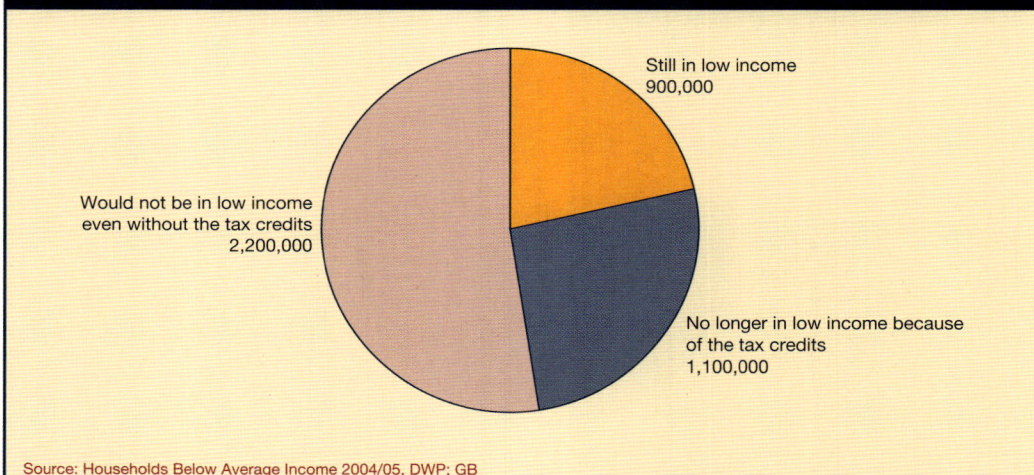

Pie chart:
- Still in low income 900,000
- No longer in low income because of the tax credits 1,100,000
- Would not be in low income even without the tax credits 2,200,000

Source: Households Below Average Income 2004/05, DWP; GB

The first graph provides an analysis of the number of children in working households where, excluding tax credits (and their predecessors), the household is in low income. For each year, it shows the number of children in three categories, namely: not in receipt of tax credits; in receipt of tax credits (over and above the family element) but still in low income; and in receipt of tax credits and, as a result, no longer in low income.

The second graph provides, for the latest year, an analysis of the children in working households in receipt of tax credits over and above the family element. The first two categories – those who are still in low income and those who, as a result of tax credits, are no longer in low income – are the same as in the first graph. The third category is children whose household would not be in low income even without tax credits.

The data for both graphs is from Households Below Average Income, based on the Family Resources Survey (FRS), and relates to Great Britain. As elsewhere, the low income threshold used is 60 per cent of contemporary median household income after deducting housing costs. To ensure comparability over time, the data for 1998/99 and earlier includes recipients of Disability Working Allowance as well as Family Credit while the data for 2003/04 onwards excludes those just receiving the family element of Child Tax Credit.

Overall adequacy of the indicator: medium. All the data is considered to be very reliable and provides reasonable estimates. However, the extensive changes in the system from year to year make the data somewhat difficult to interpret.

In workless households

10A: The number of children in workless households has fallen by a quarter over the last decade, with most of this fall being for children in couple households.

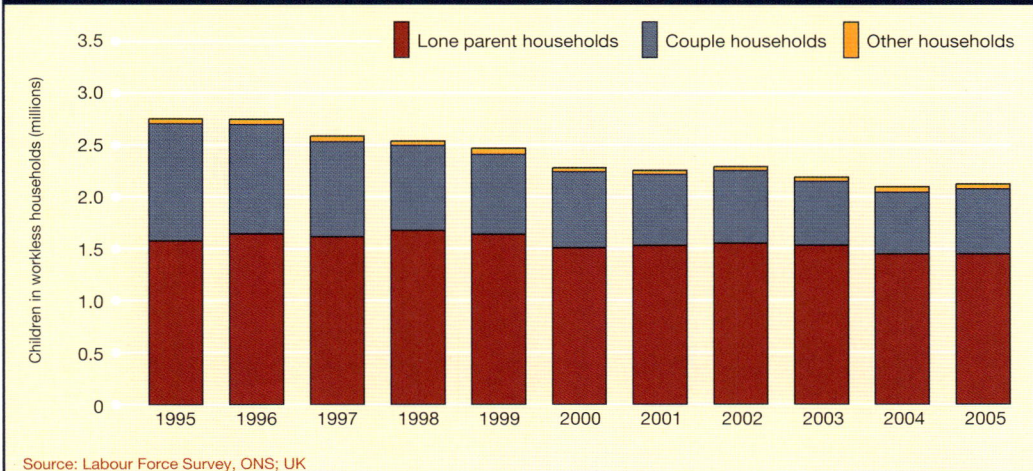

Legend: Lone parent households | Couple households | Other households

Y-axis: Children in workless households (millions)

X-axis years: 1995, 1996, 1997, 1998, 1999, 2000, 2001, 2002, 2003, 2004, 2005

Source: Labour Force Survey, ONS; UK

10B: The UK has a higher proportion of its children living in workless households than any other EU country.

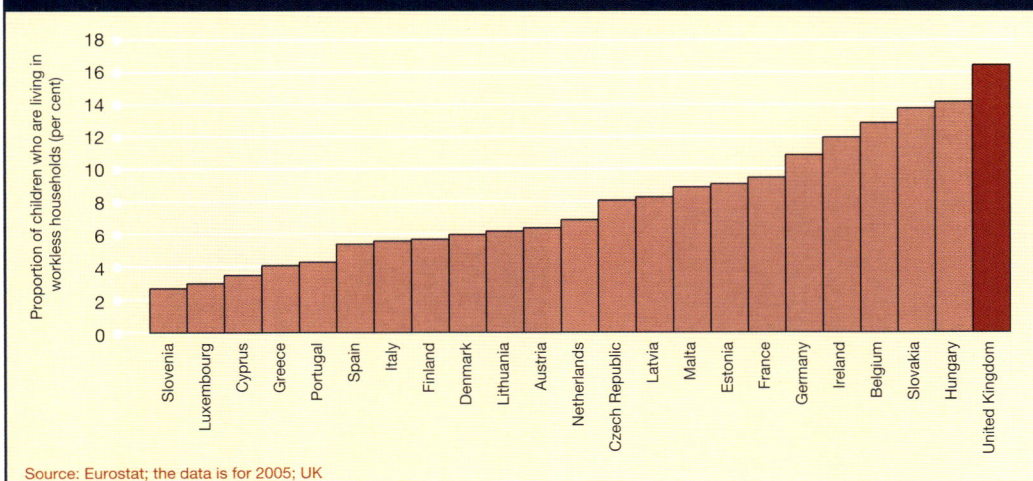

Y-axis: Proportion of children who are living in workless households (per cent)

X-axis countries: Slovenia, Luxembourg, Cyprus, Greece, Portugal, Spain, Italy, Finland, Denmark, Lithuania, Austria, Netherlands, Czech Republic, Latvia, Malta, Estonia, France, Germany, Ireland, Belgium, Slovakia, Hungary, United Kingdom

Source: Eurostat; the data is for 2005; UK

The first graph shows the number of children aged under 16 living in households in which none of the working-age adults have paid employment. The data is separated by family type, namely couple households, lone parent households and other households. The data source is the Labour Force Survey (LFS) and the data for each year is the average of the spring and autumn quarters (the data not being collected in the other two quarters). The data relates to the United Kingdom and is not seasonally adjusted. Working-age households are those with at least one person of working age. Households made up of students and those in which the head of household is retired are excluded.

The second graph shows the proportion of children aged 0-17 in each EU country who live in workless households. The data source is Eurostat, which in turn draws its data from the Labour Force Surveys in each country. The data is for the year 2005.

Overall adequacy of the indicator: high. The LFS is a large, well-established, quarterly government survey, designed to be representative of the population as a whole.

Low birthweight babies

11A: Babies born to parents from manual social backgrounds continue to be more likely to have a low birthweight than those born to parents from non-manual social backgrounds.

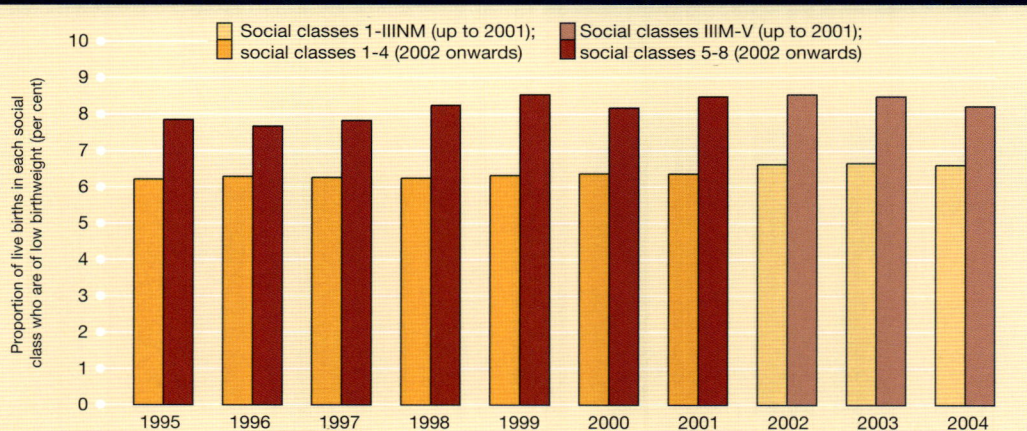

Legend:
- Social classes 1–IIINM (up to 2001); social classes 1–4 (2002 onwards)
- Social classes IIIM–V (up to 2001); social classes 5–8 (2002 onwards)

Y-axis: Proportion of live births in each social class who are of low birthweight (per cent)

X-axis years: 1995, 1996, 1997, 1998, 1999, 2000, 2001, 2002, 2003, 2004

Source: Childhood, infant and perinatal mortality statistics, DH3, ONS; England and Wales

11B: Babies born to lone parents are more likely to be of low birthweight than babies born to couples.

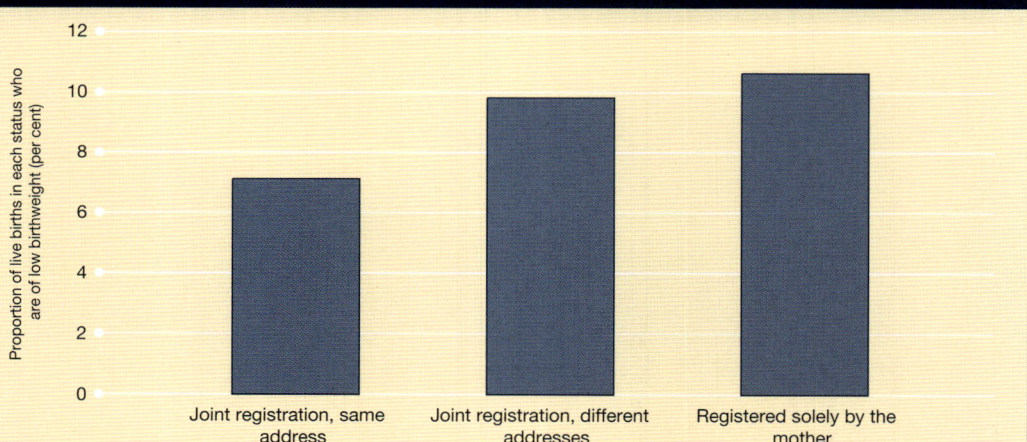

Y-axis: Proportion of live births in each status who are of low birthweight (per cent)

X-axis categories: Joint registration, same address; Joint registration, different addresses; Registered solely by the mother

Source: Childhood, infant and perinatal mortality statistics, 2004 data, DH3, ONS; England and Wales

The first graph shows the proportion of babies born each year who are defined as having a low birthweight, i.e. less than 2½ kilograms (5½ lbs). The proportions are shown separately for babies according to the social class of the father. The social class classifications for 2002 onwards are those recently introduced which range from 1 (higher managerial and professional) to 8 (never worked and long-term unemployed). The data is for live births only (i.e. it excludes stillbirths). It is based on a 10 per cent sample coded to father's occupation and excludes sole registrations by mothers.

The second graph shows, for the latest year, how the proportion of babies who are of low birthweight varies according to the parents' living status at the time of the registration of birth. The data is based on a 100 per cent count of live births.

The data source for both graphs is ONS DH3 childhood, infant and perinatal mortality statistics and relates to England and Wales.

Overall adequacy of the indicator: limited. The data itself is large and reputable, but classification by the social class of the father may be problematic since those where no details are known about the father are not included at all.

Child health

12A: While the rate of infant death among those from non-manual social backgrounds has fallen over the last decade, the pattern for those from manual social backgrounds is less clear.

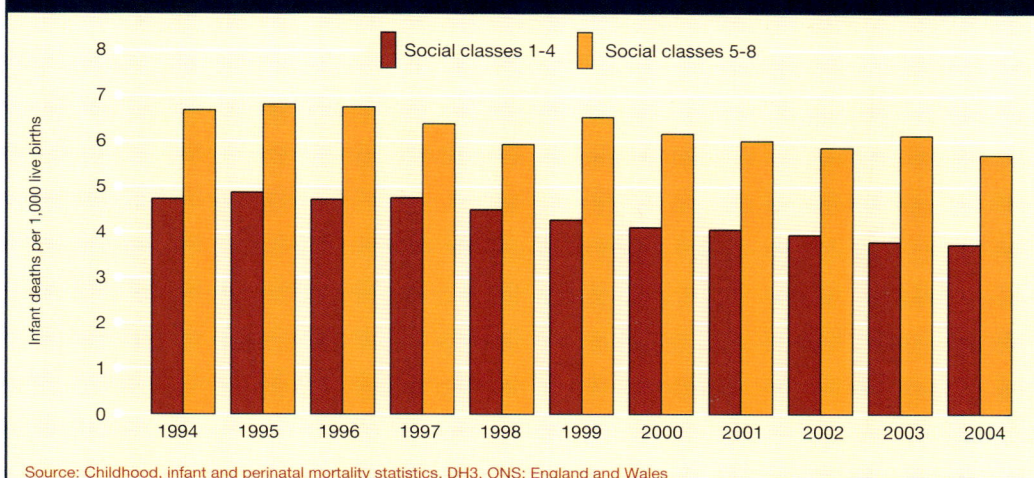

Social classes 1-4 / Social classes 5-8

Infant deaths per 1,000 live births

1994 1995 1996 1997 1998 1999 2000 2001 2002 2003 2004

Source: Childhood, infant and perinatal mortality statistics, DH3, ONS; England and Wales

12B: Children from routine and manual backgrounds have, on average, one more tooth with obvious tooth decay than other children.

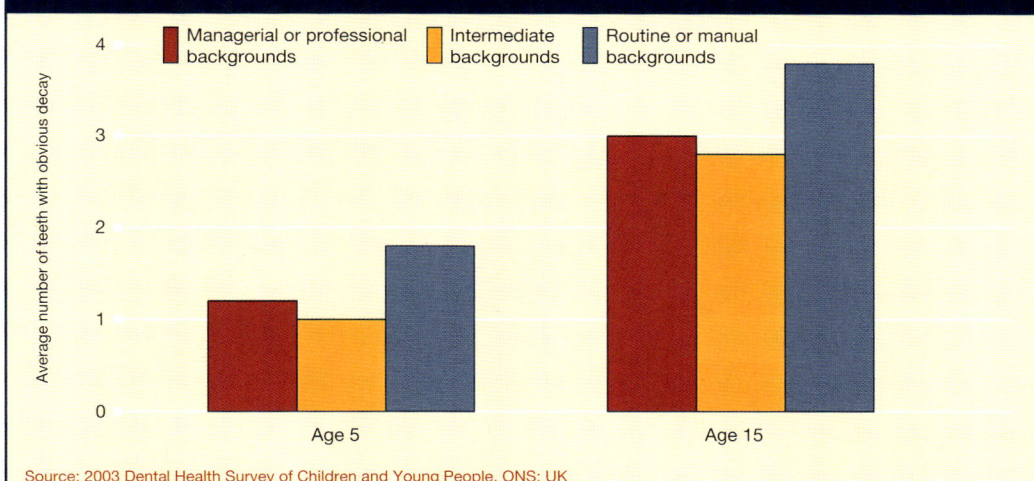

Managerial or professional backgrounds / Intermediate backgrounds / Routine or manual backgrounds

Average number of teeth with obvious decay

Age 5   Age 15

Source: 2003 Dental Health Survey of Children and Young People, ONS; UK

The first graph shows the annual number of infant deaths per 1,000 live births, with the data shown separately according to the social class of the father. Infant deaths are deaths which occur at ages under one year. The social class classifications are those recently introduced which range from 1 (higher managerial and professional) to 8 (never worked and long-term unemployed). The data source is ONS DH3 childhood, infant and perinatal mortality statistics. The data relates to England and Wales and is based on a 10 per cent sample of live births. Cases where the social class of the father is unknown have been excluded from the analysis.

The second graph shows, for both five-year-olds and 15-year-olds, how the average number of teeth with obvious tooth decay varies by the social class of their family. The data source is a 2003 government survey entitled Dental Health Survey of Children and Young People. The data relates to the United Kingdom. The choice of five-year-olds and 15-year-olds is to avoid the age group where primary teeth are being replaced by permanent teeth.

Overall adequacy of the indicator: high. The sample sizes in the first graph are substantial and relatively few (5 per cent) have not been coded to a social class.

Underage pregnancies

13A: While the number of births to girls conceiving under age 16 has fallen by a third since 1996, the number of abortions is unchanged.

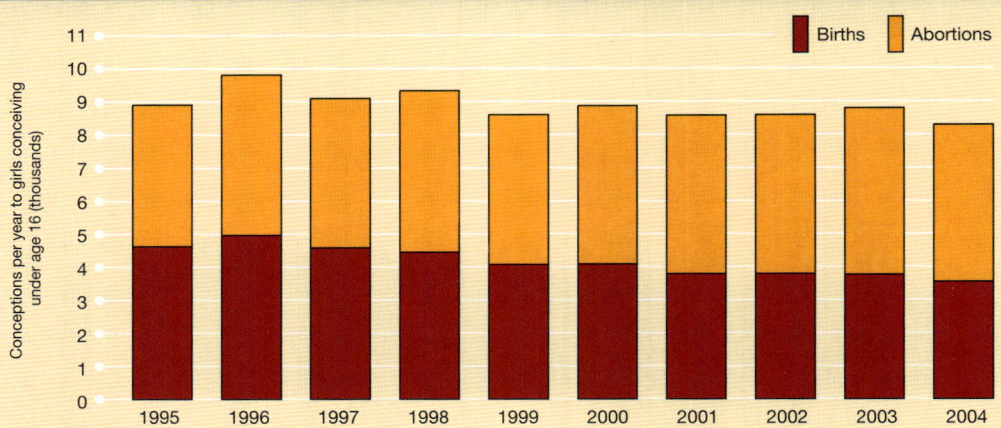

Source: Health Statistics Quarterly, ONS and ISD Scotland; GB

13B: Teenage motherhood is eight times as common amongst those from manual social backgrounds as for those from professional backgrounds.

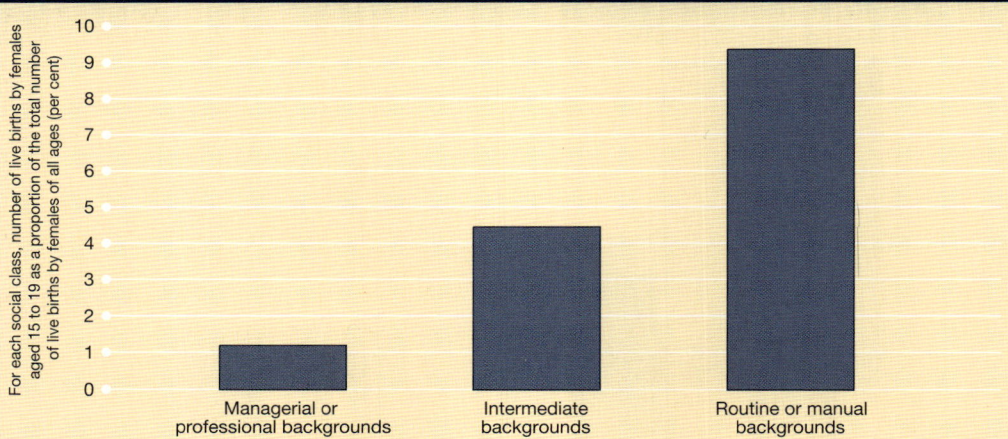

Source: Childhood, infant and perinatal mortality statistics, 2004 data, DH3, ONS; England and Wales

The first graph shows the number of conceptions a year to girls conceiving under the age of 16, with the data shown separately for delivered babies and for abortions. The data relates to Great Britain. English and Welsh conceptions leading to births are counted during the actual year of conception, while Scottish conceptions are counted after the birth of the child, which is commonly in the calendar year following conception. ONS population projections have been used for the number of 15-year-old girls.

The second graph shows, for the latest year, the number of live births by females aged 15 to 19 in each social class as a proportion of the total live births by females of that social class. The data source is the DH3 mortality statistics from ONS. The analysis is based on the recorded social class of the father of the baby. As such, it does not include the 25 per cent of births to females aged 15 to 19 which were sole registrations.

Overall adequacy of the indicator: medium. The collection of the conception and births statistics is an established process.

Low attainment at school (11-year-olds)

14A: Progress continues to be made in the literacy and numeracy of 11-year-olds – including those in deprived schools.

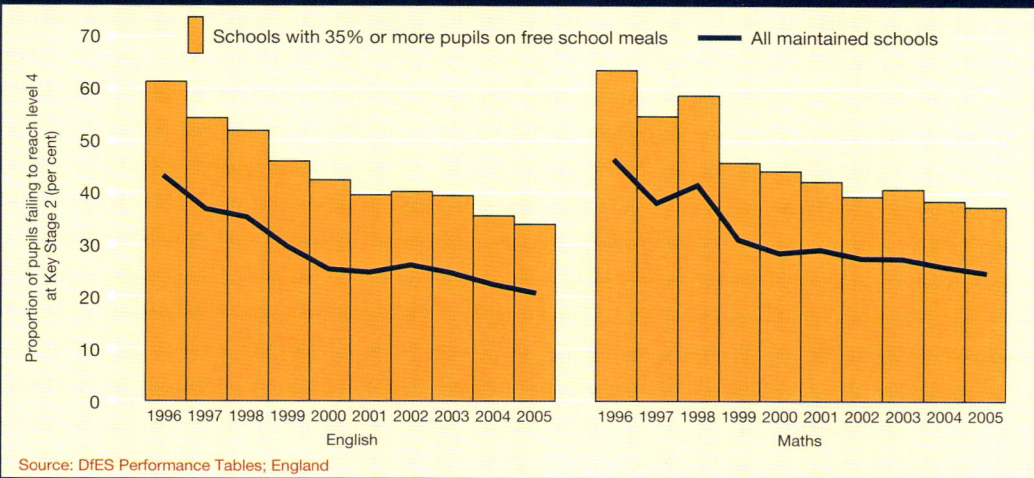

Legend: ☐ Schools with 35% or more pupils on free school meals   —— All maintained schools

y-axis: Proportion of pupils failing to reach level 4 at Key Stage 2 (per cent)

x-axis (left chart): 1996 1997 1998 1999 2000 2001 2002 2003 2004 2005 — English

x-axis (right chart): 1996 1997 1998 1999 2000 2001 2002 2003 2004 2005 — Maths

Source: DfES Performance Tables; England

14B: Differences in achievement between 11-year-old pupils with/without free school meals are greatest amongst white pupils.

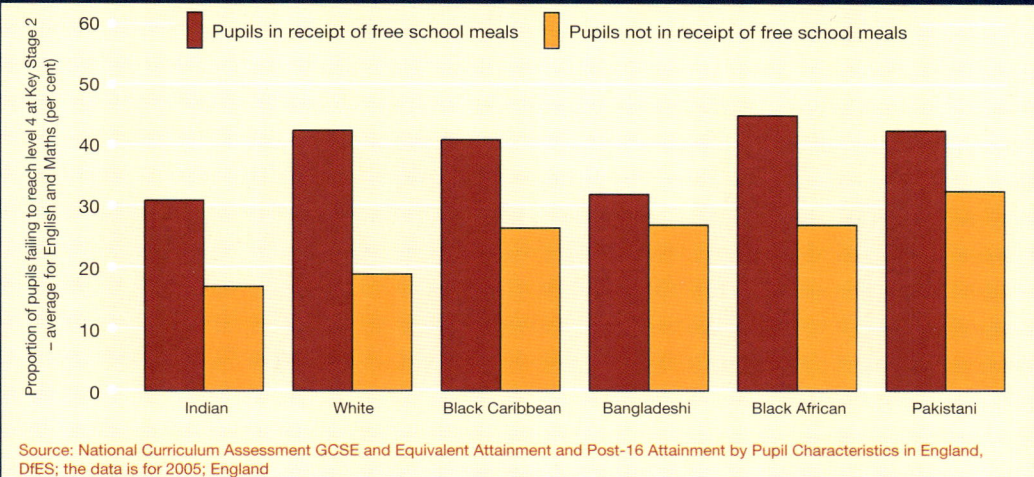

Legend: ☐ Pupils in receipt of free school meals   ☐ Pupils not in receipt of free school meals

y-axis: Proportion of pupils failing to reach level 4 at Key Stage 2 – average for English and Maths (per cent)

x-axis: Indian, White, Black Caribbean, Bangladeshi, Black African, Pakistani

Source: National Curriculum Assessment GCSE and Equivalent Attainment and Post-16 Attainment by Pupil Characteristics in England, DfES; the data is for 2005; England

The first graph compares the proportion of children failing to reach level 4 at Key Stage 2 (11 years old) in schools which have at least 35 per cent of pupils receiving free school meals with that for all maintained mainstream schools. The graph shows Maths and English separately and shows changes over time. The 35 per cent threshold is a level commonly used by the government itself when looking at examination results for schools with a high level of children with free school meals. The data source is DfES performance tables. The data relates to England and covers all local education authority maintained schools.

The second graph show how the proportion of children failing to achieve level 4 at Key Stage 2 varies by ethnicity and whether or not the pupil is in receipt of free school meals. The data source is the DfES publication called *National Curriculum Assessment GCSE and Equivalent Attainment and Post-16 Attainment by Pupil Characteristics in England*. The data relates to England and covers all maintained schools. The data is for 2005.

Overall adequacy of the indicator: medium. While the data itself is sound enough, the choice of the particular level of exam success is a matter of judgement.

Low attainment at school (16-year-olds)

15A: One in ten 16-year-olds still obtain fewer than 5 GCSEs, the same as in 1999/00. This lack of improvement contrasts with the continuing improvement for the higher threshold of 5 GCSEs at grade C or above.

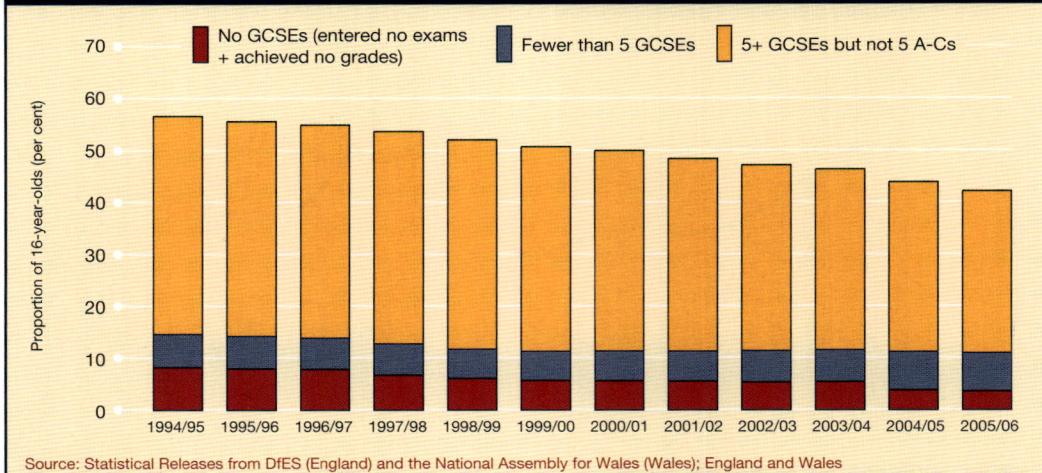

Legend:
- No GCSEs (entered no exams + achieved no grades)
- Fewer than 5 GCSEs
- 5+ GCSEs but not 5 A-Cs

Y-axis: Proportion of 16-year-olds (per cent)

X-axis: 1994/95, 1995/96, 1996/97, 1997/98, 1998/99, 1999/00, 2000/01, 2001/02, 2002/03, 2003/04, 2004/05, 2005/06

Source: Statistical Releases from DfES (England) and the National Assembly for Wales (Wales); England and Wales

15B: Three-quarters of white pupils in receipt of free school meals do not obtain 5 or more GCSEs at grade C or above.

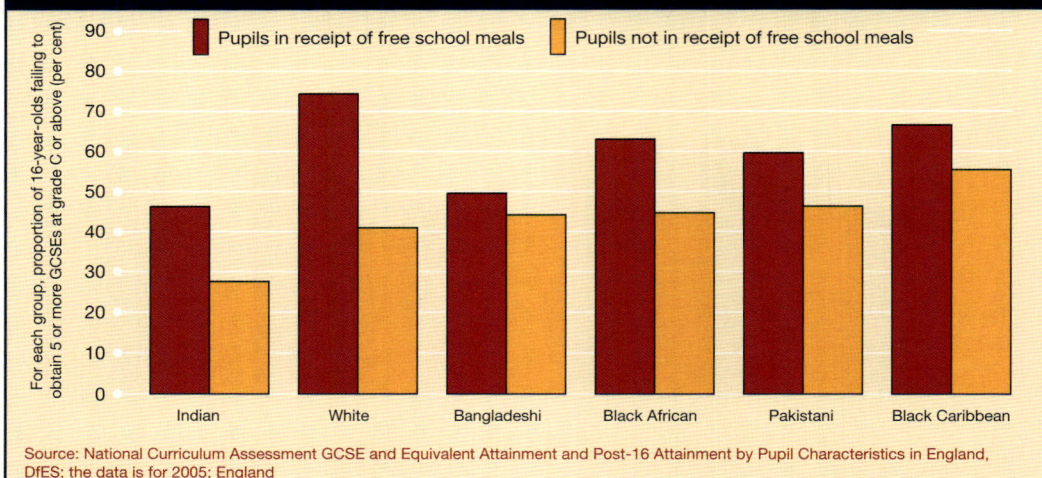

Legend:
- Pupils in receipt of free school meals
- Pupils not in receipt of free school meals

Y-axis: For each group, proportion of 16-year-olds failing to obtain 5 or more GCSEs at grade C or above (per cent)

X-axis: Indian, White, Bangladeshi, Black African, Pakistani, Black Caribbean

Source: National Curriculum Assessment GCSE and Equivalent Attainment and Post-16 Attainment by Pupil Characteristics in England, DfES; the data is for 2005; England

The first graph shows the proportion of students (defined as pupils aged 15 at 31 August in the calendar year prior to sitting the exams) failing to obtain five or more GCSEs at grade C or above in England and Wales. The data is split between those who obtain no GCSE grades at all (either because they do not enter for exams or achieve no passes), those who do obtain some GCSEs but less than five, and those who obtain five or more GCSEs but less than five at grade C or above. The data sources are DfES and the Welsh Assembly. The data relates to England and Wales and covers all schools including city technology colleges and academies, community and foundation special schools, hospital schools, pupil referral units and non-maintained special schools.

The second graph shows how the proportion of children failing to achieve five or more GCSEs at grade C or above varies by ethnicity and whether or not the pupil is in receipt of free school meals. The data source is the DfES publication called *National Curriculum Assessment GCSE and Equivalent Attainment and Post-16 Attainment by Pupil Characteristics in England*. The data relates to England and covers all maintained schools. The data is for 2005.

Overall adequacy of the indicator: medium. While the data itself is sound enough, the choice of the particular level of exam success is a matter of judgement.

School exclusions

16A: The number of permanent exclusions has remained broadly unchanged over the last five years.

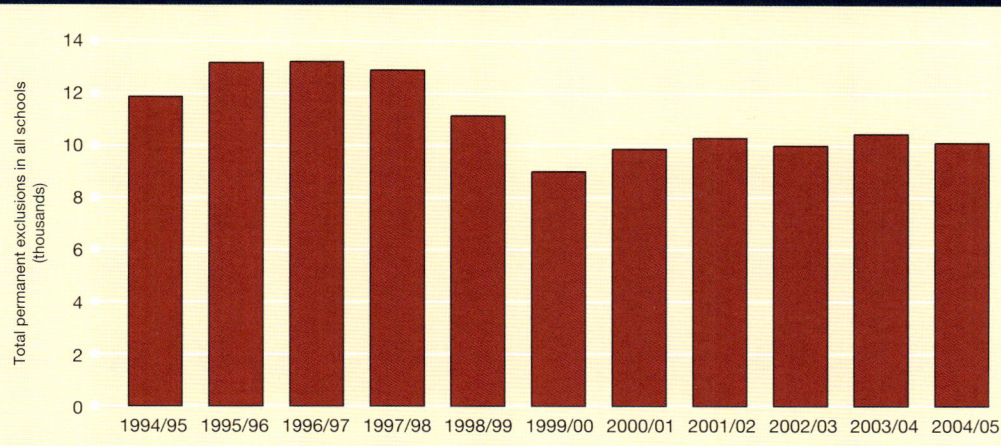

Y-axis: Total permanent exclusions in all schools (thousands)

Bars (approx values): 1994/95 ≈ 11.8; 1995/96 ≈ 13.2; 1996/97 ≈ 13.2; 1997/98 ≈ 12.9; 1998/99 ≈ 11.1; 1999/00 ≈ 9.0; 2000/01 ≈ 9.8; 2001/02 ≈ 10.2; 2002/03 ≈ 9.9; 2003/04 ≈ 10.3; 2004/05 ≈ 10.0

Sources: DfES Statistical Bulletin; National Assembly for Wales; Scottish Executive; GB

16B: Despite substantial reductions in recent years, black Caribbean pupils are still three times as likely to be excluded from school as white pupils.

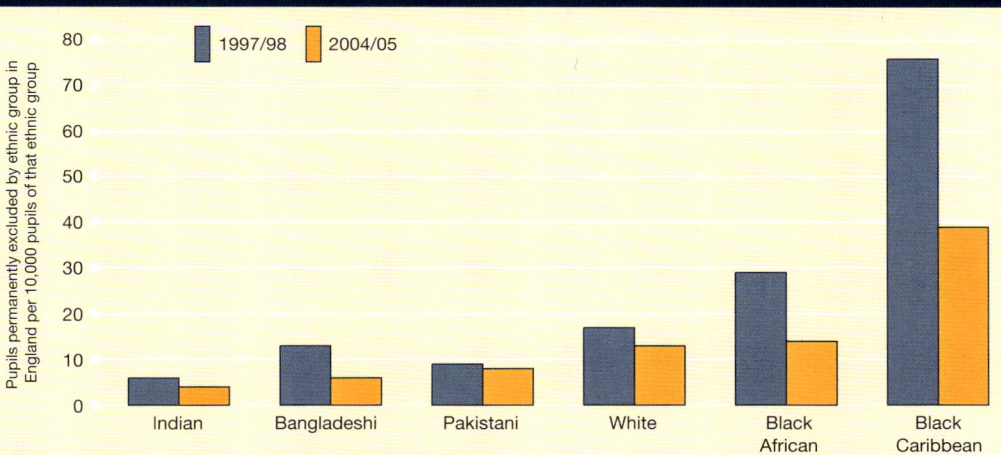

Y-axis: Pupils permanently excluded by ethnic group in England per 10,000 pupils of that ethnic group

Legend: 1997/98, 2004/05

Categories: Indian, Bangladeshi, Pakistani, White, Black African, Black Caribbean

Source: Permanent exclusions from schools, England, DfES; England

The first graph shows the number of pupils permanently excluded from primary, secondary and special schools. The data relates to Great Britain. In Scotland, the data (referred to as 'removals from register') was collected from local authorities via a new survey from 1998/99. Previously, this information had been collected from individual schools. Data from 1994/95 to 1997/98 for Scotland is therefore not strictly comparable with the more recent figures.

The second graph shows how, for the latest year, the rate of permanent exclusions varies for children from different ethnic backgrounds. The data relates to England only.

Overall adequacy of the indicator: medium. Exclusions are susceptible to administrative procedures; for example, these officially recorded numbers may well under-represent the true number of exclusions if parents are persuaded to withdraw their child rather than have the school exclude them.

Chapter 3
Young adults

Young adults

This chapter has three themes containing six indicators in total. The themes are:

- transitions to adulthood;

- economic circumstances;

- health and well-being.

Transitions to adulthood

Choice of indicators

The three indicators here cover a number of quite different aspects of transition from childhood to adulthood and from education to work.

The first indicator shows how the proportion of 19-year-olds with either no qualifications or very limited ones has changed over time. The supporting graph shows how the proportion with various levels of qualification varies by age, from the age of 16 to the age of 25.

The second indicator looks at 16-year-olds who are in neither education nor training. The first graph shows trend over time whilst the supporting graph provides a further breakdown by ethnic group.

The third graph shows the number of 18- to 20-year-olds found guilty of an indictable offence and how that number has changed over the last decade. The supporting graph shows the proportion of 16- to 20-year-olds in prison for different ethnic groups.

What the indicators show

Indicator 17 Without a basic qualification

One in four 19-year-olds still fail to achieve a basic level of qualification and up to one in ten have no qualifications at all.

Most 19-year-olds without NVQ2 or its academic equivalent (e.g. 5 or more good GCSEs) still lack such qualifications at age 25.

Indicator 18 School leavers

One in six of all 16-year-olds are not in education or training. This proportion has not fallen since 2000.

The proportion of white 16-year-olds no longer in full-time education is higher than that for any minority ethnic group, but many are undertaking some form of training.

Indicator 19 With a criminal record

The number of 18- to 20-year-olds found guilty of an indictable offence has been falling steadily over the last few years and is now a quarter lower than in 1999.

Black young adults are three times as likely as white young adults to be in prison.

Economic circumstances

Choice of indicators

The first indicator is concerned with lack of paid work among young adults, while the second indicator is concerned with the prevalence of low pay. In each case, the first graph compares the situation for young adults with that for older adults and the second graph compares the prospects for young adults with different levels of educational qualification. By covering the 25 to 29 age group in the two supporting graphs, they show the connection between educational outcomes in late teens and future economic prospects.

What the indicators show

Indicator 20 Unemployment

The unemployment rate for 18- to 24-year-olds has fallen by a quarter over the last decade. But it is now three times the rate for older workers, which has halved over the same period.

The lower a young adult's qualifications, the more likely they are to be lacking but wanting paid work.

Indicator 21 Low pay

Between the ages of 18 and 21, more than half of all full-time employees are paid less than £6.50 an hour. This is in sharp contrast to those aged 22 and over.

The lower a young adult's qualifications, the more likely they are to be low paid.

Health and well-being

Choice of indicators

Data on social exclusion among young adults is very limited. In this context, the sole indicator here relates to suicides. The first graph shows trends over time, with the supporting graph showing risks by social class.

What the indicators show

Indicator 22 Suicides

The number of suicides amongst young adults aged 15 to 24 has fallen by a third since its peak in 1997.

Young men from routine and manual backgrounds are twice as likely to commit suicide as those from intermediate backgrounds and three times as likely as those from professional and managerial backgrounds.

Without a basic qualification

17A: One in four 19-year-olds still fail to achieve a basic level of qualification and up to one in ten have no qualifications at all.

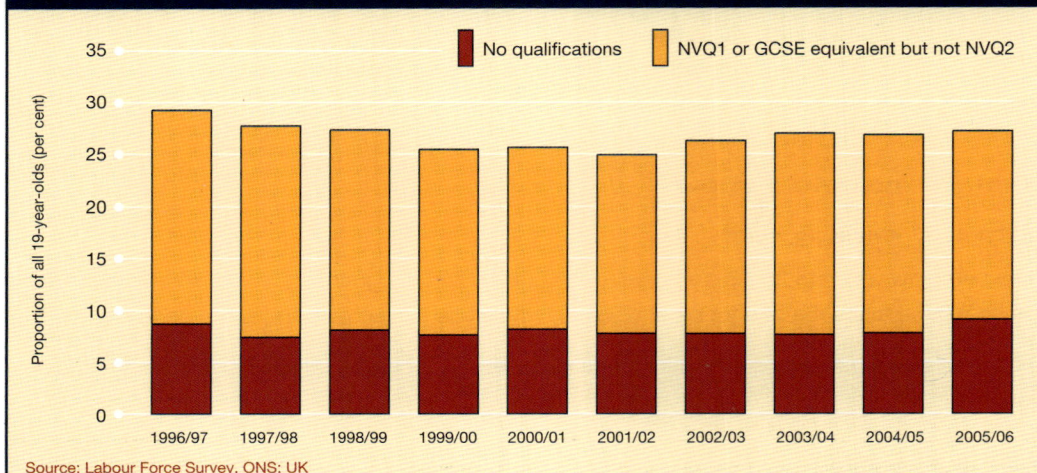

Legend: No qualifications | NVQ1 or GCSE equivalent but not NVQ2

Y-axis: Proportion of all 19-year-olds (per cent) — 0 to 35

X-axis: 1996/97, 1997/98, 1998/99, 1999/00, 2000/01, 2001/02, 2002/03, 2003/04, 2004/05, 2005/06

Source: Labour Force Survey, ONS; UK

17B: Most 19-year-olds without NVQ2 or its academic equivalent (e.g. 5 or more good GCSEs) still lack such qualifications at age 25.

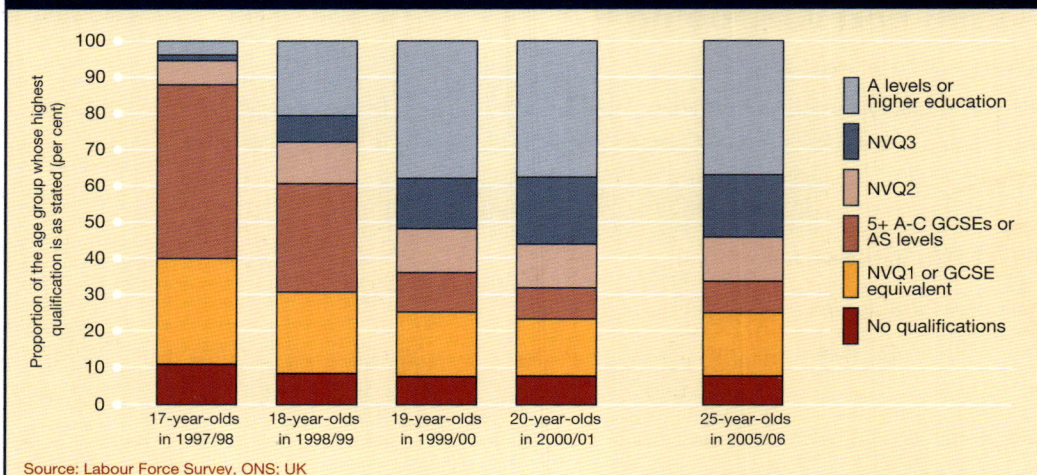

Y-axis: Proportion of the age group whose highest qualification is as stated (per cent) — 0 to 100

X-axis: 17-year-olds in 1997/98, 18-year-olds in 1998/99, 19-year-olds in 1999/00, 20-year-olds in 2000/01, 25-year-olds in 2005/06

Legend:
- A levels or higher education
- NVQ3
- NVQ2
- 5+ A-C GCSEs or AS levels
- NVQ1 or GCSE equivalent
- No qualifications

Source: Labour Force Survey, ONS; UK

The first graph shows the proportion of 19-year-olds without a basic qualification, with the data shown separately for those without NVQ2 or equivalent and those without any GCSEs at grade G or above. DfES equivalence scales have been used to translate academic qualifications into their vocational equivalents. So, for example, 'NVQ2 or equivalent' includes those with five GCSEs at grade C or above, GNVQ level 2, two AS levels or one A level. In line with these equivalence scales, 35 per cent of those with an 'other qualification' are considered to have NVQ2 or equivalent and a further 10 per cent are considered to have NVQ3 or equivalent.

The second graph shows how the proportion of young adults with various levels of highest qualification varies by age. The levels of qualification shown are a mixture of academic and vocational qualifications, namely A level or higher education, NVQ3, NVQ2, 5+ A-C GCSEs or AS levels, NVQ1 or GCSE equivalent, and no qualifications. The ages shown are 17 to 25.

The data source for both graphs is the Labour Force Survey (LFS) and relates to the United Kingdom.

Overall adequacy of the indicator: high. The LFS is a well-established survey designed to be representative of the population as whole.

School leavers

18A: One in six of all 16-year-olds are not in education or training. This proportion has not fallen since 2000.

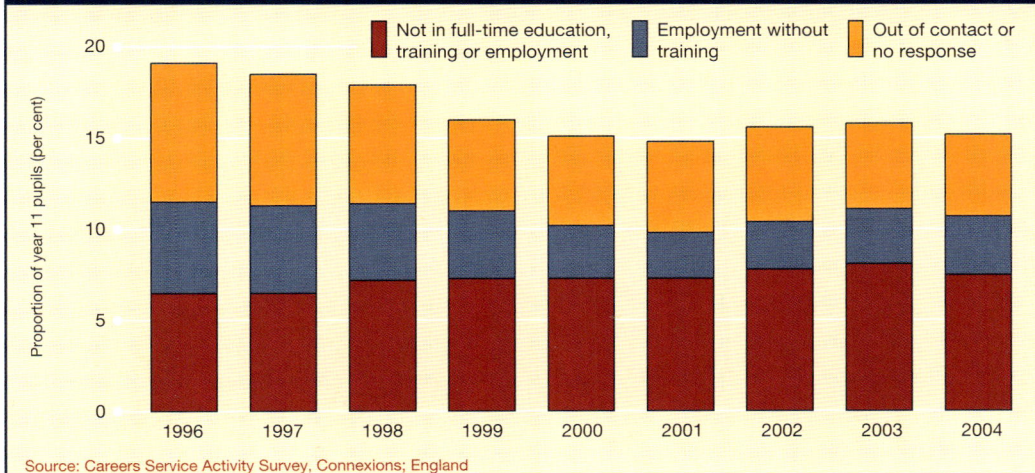

Legend:
- Not in full-time education, training or employment
- Employment without training
- Out of contact or no response

Y-axis: Proportion of year 11 pupils (per cent)

X-axis years: 1996, 1997, 1998, 1999, 2000, 2001, 2002, 2003, 2004

Source: Careers Service Activity Survey, Connexions; England

18B: The proportion of white 16-year-olds no longer in full-time education is higher than that for any ethnic minority, but many are undertaking some form of training.

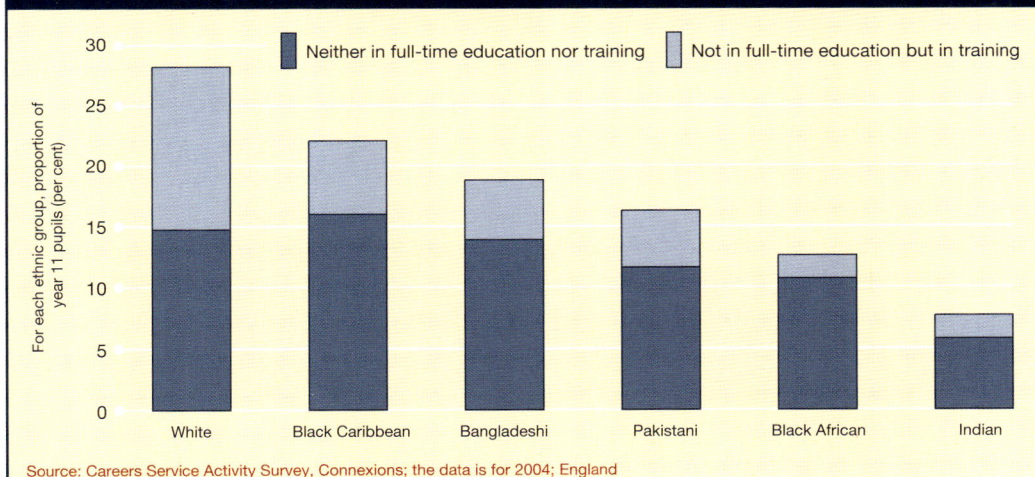

Legend:
- Neither in full-time education nor training
- Not in full-time education but in training

Y-axis: For each ethnic group, proportion of year 11 pupils (per cent)

X-axis categories: White, Black Caribbean, Bangladeshi, Pakistani, Black African, Indian

Source: Careers Service Activity Survey, Connexions; the data is for 2004; England

The first graph shows the proportion of year 11 pupils who are not in full-time education or training.

The second graph shows, for the latest year, how the proportions who are not in full-time education vary by ethnic group.

The data source for both graphs is the Connexions Careers Service Activity Survey and the data relates to England only. 'Out of contact or no response' effectively means that the Connexions service has lost contact with the person. In the ethnic group analysis, any operational area which shows a proportion of 'ethnicity not known' of more than 11 per cent is excluded from the analysis.

Overall adequacy of the indicator: high. The Careers Service Activity Survey is a well-established government survey, although no survey appears to have been undertaken since 2004.

With a criminal record

19A: The number of 18- to 20-year-olds found guilty of an indictable offence has been falling steadily over the last few years and is now a quarter lower than in 1999.

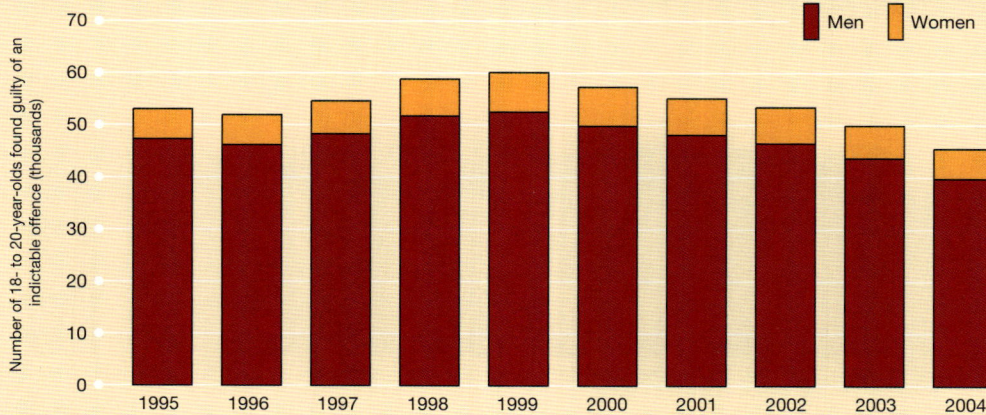

Number of 18- to 20-year-olds found guilty of an indictable offence (thousands)

Men   Women

1995 1996 1997 1998 1999 2000 2001 2002 2003 2004

Source: Criminal Statistics England and Wales, Home Office; England and Wales

19B: Black young adults are three times as likely as white young adults to be in prison.

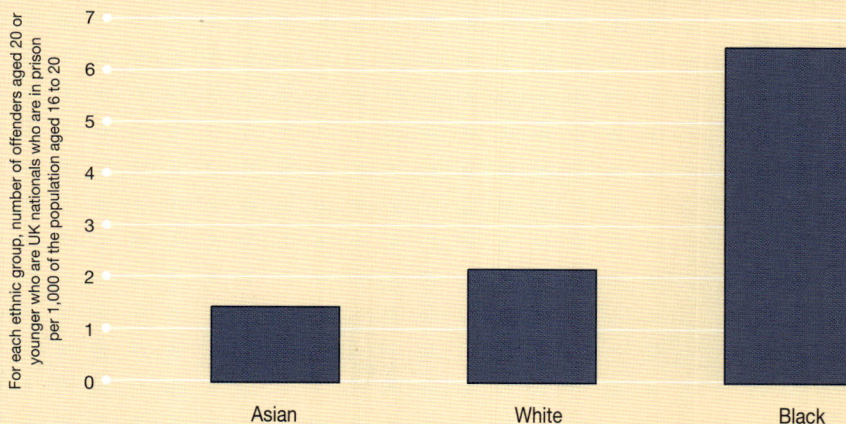

For each ethnic group, number of offenders aged 20 or younger who are UK nationals who are in prison per 1,000 of the population aged 16 to 20

Asian   White   Black

Source: Offender Management Caseload Statistics, Home Office; the data is for June 2005; England and Wales

The first graph shows the number of young men and women aged 18 to 20 who were convicted of an indictable offence in each year. The data source is the Home Office's Criminal Statistics for England and Wales.

The second graph shows, for the latest year, the likelihood of being in prison under sentence across different ethnic groups. These likelihoods are expressed in terms of the number of offenders aged 20 or younger sentenced who are UK nationals and were in prison in June 2005 per 1,000 population aged 16 to 20 of the relevant ethnic group. The data source is the Home Office Prison Statistics for England and Wales. The figures are for UK nationals only and therefore exclude foreign nationals, with it being assumed that the prison proportion who are foreign nationals is similar for the 16 to 20 age group as for the all-age proportions. The population estimates are from the 2001 Census, with those of mixed race being included in the relevant ethnic minority group.

Overall adequacy of the indicator: medium. The data is dependent upon administrative practices of the police and the judicial system.

Unemployment

20A: The unemployment rate for 18- to 24-year-olds has fallen by a quarter over the last decade. But it is now three times the rate for older workers, which has halved over the same period.

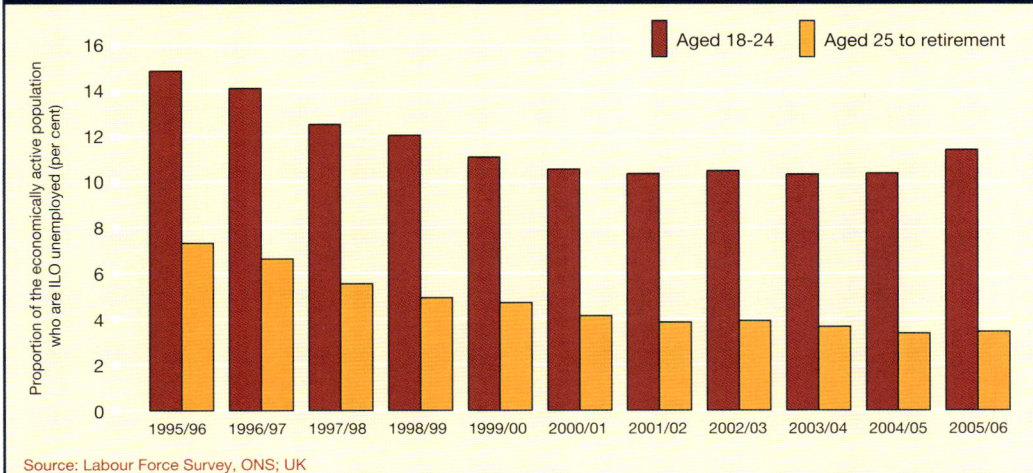

Legend: Aged 18-24 | Aged 25 to retirement

Y-axis: Proportion of the economically active population who are ILO unemployed (per cent)

X-axis categories: 1995/96, 1996/97, 1997/98, 1998/99, 1999/00, 2000/01, 2001/02, 2002/03, 2003/04, 2004/05, 2005/06

Source: Labour Force Survey, ONS; UK

20B: The lower a young adult's qualifications, the more likely they are to be lacking but wanting paid work.

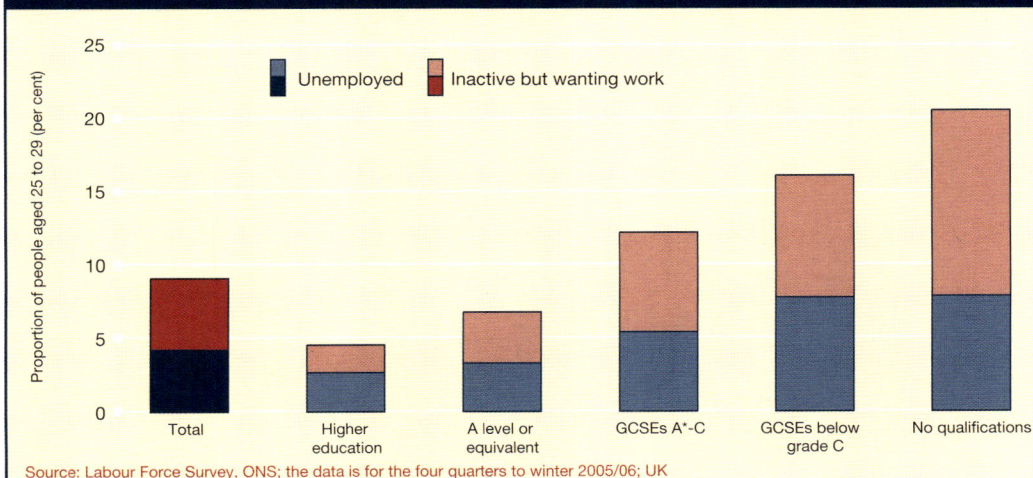

Legend: Unemployed | Inactive but wanting work

Y-axis: Proportion of people aged 25 to 29 (per cent)

X-axis categories: Total, Higher education, A level or equivalent, GCSEs A*-C, GCSEs below grade C, No qualifications

Source: Labour Force Survey, ONS; the data is for the four quarters to winter 2005/06; UK

The first graph shows the unemployment rate for those aged 18 to 24, compared with those aged 25 and over (up to retirement). 'Unemployment' is the ILO definition and includes all those with no paid work in the survey week who were available to start work in the next fortnight and who either looked for work in the last month or were waiting to start a job already obtained. The ILO unemployment rate is the proportion of the economically active population who are unemployed on the ILO measure (i.e. the total population for the relevant age group less those classified as economically inactive). So, for example, it excludes those still in education.

The second graph shows the proportion of 25- to 29-year-olds who lack but want paid work, with the data broken down by level of highest qualification. The data is shown separately for those who are unemployed and those counted as 'economically inactive' who nevertheless want paid work. This latter group includes people not available to start work for some time and those not actively seeking work. The lower age limit of 25 has been chosen on the grounds that a) the vast majority of people will have completed their formal education by that age and b) they will no longer be in casual employment (as, for example, students often are).

The data source for both graphs is the Labour Force Survey (LFS) and relates to the United Kingdom.

Overall adequacy of the indicator: high. The LFS is a large, well-established, quarterly government survey designed to be representative of the population as a whole.

Low pay

21A: Between the ages of 18 and 21, more than half of all full-time employees are paid less than £6.50 per hour. This is in sharp contrast to those aged 22 and over.

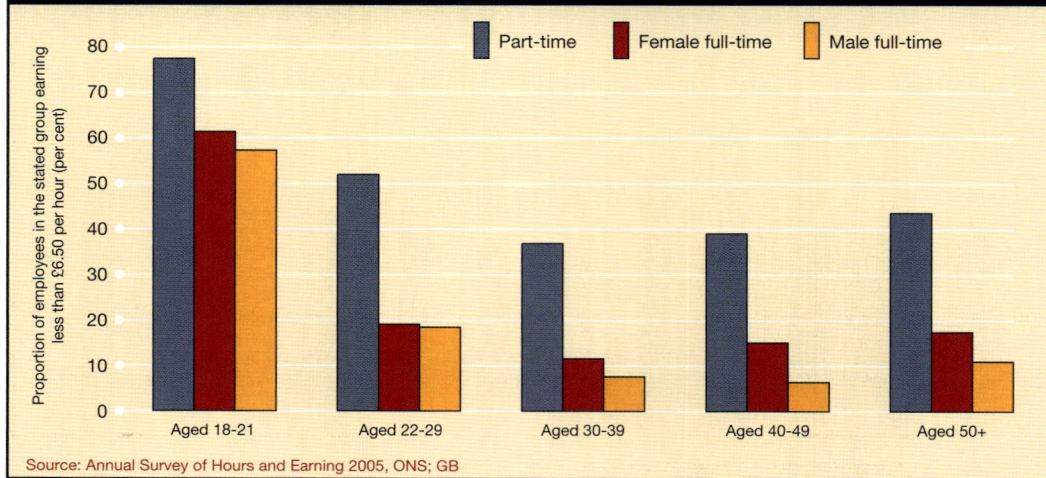

Source: Annual Survey of Hours and Earning 2005, ONS; GB

21B: The lower a young adult's qualifications, the more likely they are to be low paid.

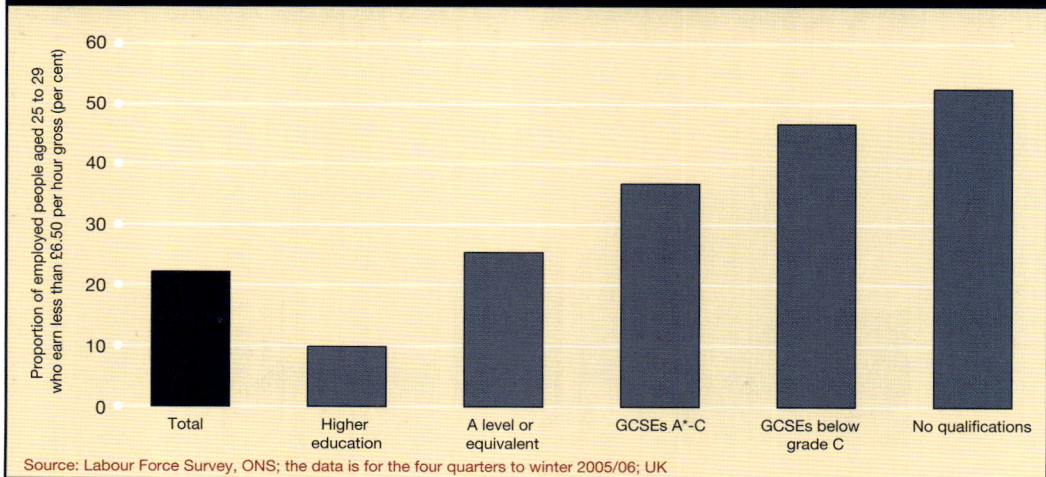

Source: Labour Force Survey, ONS; the data is for the four quarters to winter 2005/06; UK

The first graph shows, for 2005, the proportions of employees paid less than £6.50 an hour by age group, with the data shown separately for part-time workers, full-time women and full-time men. The data source is the Annual Survey of Hours and Earnings (ASHE) and relates to the United Kingdom. The threshold of £6.50 an hour has been chosen as being roughly two-thirds of the Great Britain median hourly earnings at the time and is commonly used as a threshold when analysing low pay.

The second graph shows the proportion of 25- to 29-year-olds who are in employment who have an average hourly gross pay of less than £6.50, with the data broken down by level of highest qualification. The lower age limit of 25 has been chosen on the grounds that a) the vast majority of people will have completed their formal education by that age and b) they will no longer be in casual employment (as, for example, students often are). The data source is the Labour Force Survey (LFS) and relates to the United Kingdom. Respondents who did not answer the questions required to perform the analysis have been excluded from the graph.

Overall adequacy of the indicator: medium. The LFS and ASHE are well-established government surveys, designed to be representative of the population as a whole. However, the data in the second graph is considered by ONS to be less reliable than that in the first graph.

Suicides

22A: The number of suicides amongst young adults aged 15 to 24 has fallen by a third since its peak in 1997.

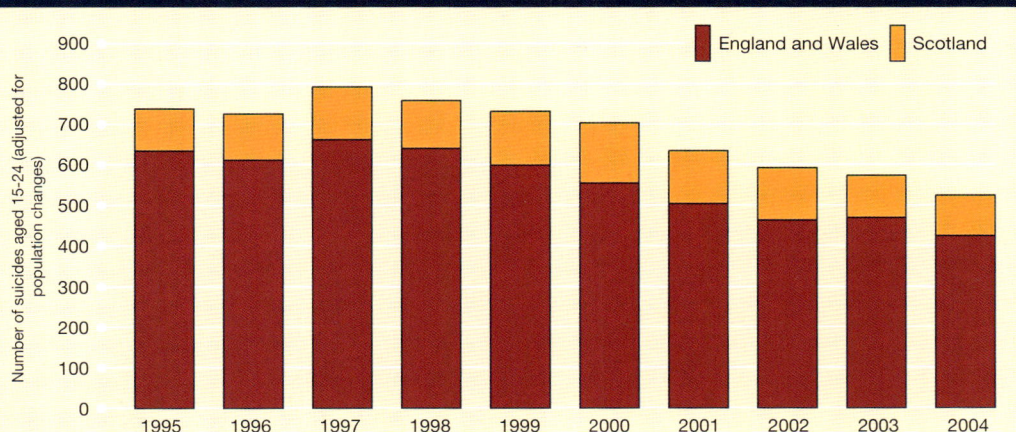

Source: ONS Mortality Division and the General Register Office for Scotland; GB

22B: Young men from routine and manual backgrounds are twice as likely to commit suicide as those from intermediate backgrounds and three times as likely as those from professional and managerial backgrounds.

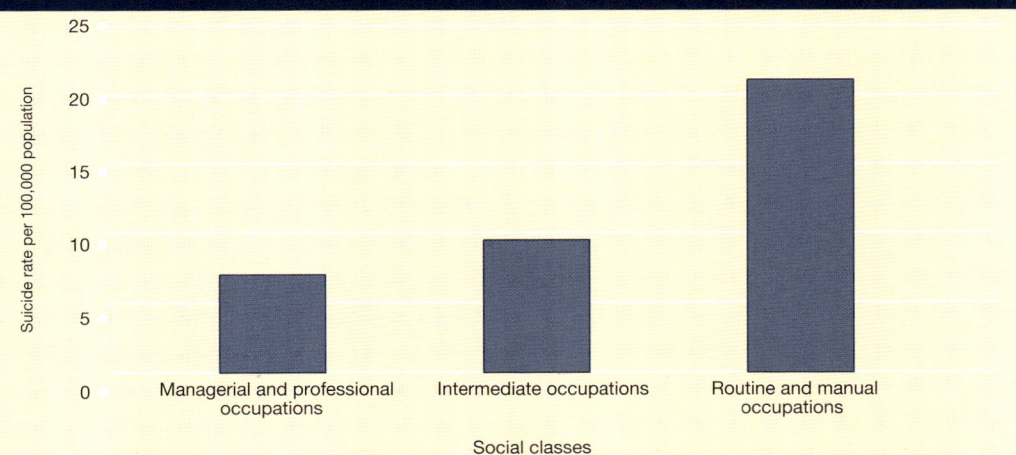

Source: Mortality Statistics Division, ONS; data is the average for 2001 to 2003; England and Wales

The first graph shows the number of suicides in Great Britain, showing the statistics separately for England and Wales and for Scotland. The figures have been adjusted for population changes over the period using ONS population estimates for each year. Suicide data includes deaths recorded as 'undetermined', where there is an open verdict, and therefore includes deaths where suicide was the probable verdict as well as those where suicide was formally given as the verdict. The data for England and Wales is based on year of occurrence whereas that for Scotland is based on year of registration but, according to ONS, is comparable with year of occurrence data for England and Wales because of the relative lack of delay between occurrence and recording in Scotland.

The second graph relates to England and Wales only. It shows the suicide rate per 100,000 for men aged 15 to 24 broken down by social class. To improve its statistical reliability, the data is the average for the years 2001 to 2003.

Overall adequacy of indicator: medium. Classification of a death as suicide depends upon the practices of coroners' courts and is therefore potentially affected by administrative or procedural changes.

Chapter 4
Working-age adults

Indicators

Economic circumstances

23 Low income and work

24 Low income and disability

25 Low income and council tax

26 Concentrations of low income

Exclusion from work

27 Wanting paid work

28 Work and disadvantaged groups

29 Workless households

Low pay

30 Low pay by gender

31 Low pay by industry

32 Pay inequalities

Disadvantaged at work

33 Insecure at work

34 Support at work

Health and well-being

35 Premature death

36 Limiting long-standing illness

37 Mental health

Working-age adults

This chapter has five themes containing 15 indicators in total. The themes are:

■ economic circumstances;

■ exclusion from work;

■ low pay;

■ disadvantaged at work;

■ health and well-being.

Economic circumstances

Choice of indicators

The first indicator focuses on how the likelihood of being in income poverty varies according to the work status of the household. The first graph shows how the risks of being in low income have changed over time, with the supporting graph showing how the absolute numbers in low income have changed over time.

The second indicator contrasts the situation of disabled and non-disabled adults as far as income poverty is concerned. The first graph shows how the proportion of each group in low income households has changed over time. The supporting graph shows how the proportion varies between disabled and non-disabled people according to the work status of the household they live in.

The third indicator looks at people who are in low income but who are nevertheless paying full Council Tax. The stimulus for this indicator is the observation that many working-age people become liable for Council Tax at much lower levels of income than apply to Income Tax. The first graph shows trends over time, while the supporting graph provides a further breakdown by age group.

The final indicator presents information on the degree to which low income working-age households are concentrated in a relatively small number of local areas and the degree to which they are therefore surrounded by other people on low income. In the absence of small area data on incomes, it uses the best available proxy, namely people in receipt of out-of-work benefits.

What the indicators show

Indicator 23 Low income and work

An adult's risk of low income varies greatly depending on how much paid work the household does. These risks have increased somewhat for all household types since the mid-1990s.

Among those aged 25 to retirement in low income households, the number who are in working households has been rising while the number who are in workless ones has been falling.

Indicator 24 Low income and disability

Disabled adults are twice as likely to live in low income households as non-disabled adults, and the gap has grown over the last decade.

Disabled people in workless households are somewhat less likely to be in low income than their non-disabled counterparts.

Indicator 25 Low income and Council Tax

More than half of all low income households are paying full Council Tax, noticeably higher than in the mid-1990s.

1½ million children in England and Wales are living in low income households where the household is paying full Council Tax.

Indicator 26 Concentrations of low income

30 per cent of working-age people receive out-of-work benefits in the areas with the highest concentrations. This compares with 10 per cent in areas with average concentrations.

Around 40 per cent of working-age recipients of key out-of-work benefits live in a fifth of small areas, while the other 60 per cent live outside of these areas.

Exclusion from work

Choice of indicators

The first indicator focuses on the number of people aged 25 to retirement who are either unemployed or economically inactive but wanting work (which together make up those described as 'lacking but wanting work'). The first graph shows the proportions for each group for each of the last 10 years, with a further breakdown by long- and short-term unemployment. The supporting graph breaks down all those 'lacking but wanting work' into the number who are unemployed and the numbers who are economically inactive by the reason for it.

The second indicator covers two of the main groups of the population where work rates are relatively low, namely disabled people and lone parents. The first graph shows trends over time. As this graph shows, the work rates for disabled people are particularly low and the trend is less favourable than for lone parents. In this context, the supporting graph shows the proportion 'lacking but wanting work' separately for disabled and non-disabled people, according to their highest level of qualification.

The third indicator focuses on workless households. The first graph shows, over time, the proportions of all working-age households who are workless according to whether they are single adult households or not and also according to whether the households have children living in them. The second graph compares the proportion of households who are workless in the United Kingdom with the rest of the European Union.

What the indicators show

Indicator 27 Wanting paid work

Whereas the number officially unemployed has halved over the last decade, with particularly large falls in long-term unemployment, the number who are 'economically inactive' but want work has only fallen by a tenth.

A third of those wanting paid work are unemployed. A further quarter are long-term sick or disabled.

Indicator 28 Work and disadvantaged groups

While the proportion of lone parents who are in paid work has increased a lot, the proportion of disabled people who are in paid work has only increased slightly.

At all levels of qualification, the proportion of people with a work-limiting disability who lack but want paid work is much greater than for those without a work-limiting disability.

Indicator 29 Workless households

While the number of 2+ adult working-age households who are workless has fallen, the number of single adult households who are workless has not.

The UK has a higher proportion of its working-age population living in workless households than most other EU countries.

Low pay

Choice of indicators

Throughout this theme and elsewhere, low pay is defined as £6.50 an hour or less in 2005. £6.50 an hour is roughly two-thirds of the Great Britain median hourly earnings and is commonly used as a threshold when analysing low pay. Where changes over time are examined, this threshold is adjusted in line with the average change in earnings over the period.

The first indicator shows the principal statistics on the extent of low pay, separately for men and women. The first graph shows the numbers of low paid men and women for each year since 1998. The supporting graph provides a further breakdown by full-and part-time employment as well as gender.

The second indicator looks at low pay by industry sectors such as retail, the public sector and manufacturing. The first graph shows the proportions of all workers in each sector who are low paid, with men and women shown separately. The supporting graph shows what share of the total number of low paid employees each sector takes.

The third indicator looks at pay inequalities, both between the top and the bottom and between men and women. The first graph compares the trends over the last decade, with the supporting graph showing the distribution of pay for each combination of full- and part-time employment and gender.

What the indicators show

Indicator 30 Low pay by gender

The proportion of employees aged 22 and over who are low paid has fallen by around a fifth over the last five years. In 2005, 30 per cent of the women – and 15 per cent of the men – were paid less than £6.50 an hour.

Around half of those paid less than £6.50 an hour are part-time workers, mainly women.

Indicator 31 Low pay by industry

Around half of employees aged 25 and over in the hotels & restaurants and wholesale & retail sectors earn less than £6.50 an hour. In both sectors, two-thirds of these people are women.

More than a quarter of all employees aged 25 to retirement earning less than £6.50 an hour work in the public sector.

Indicator 32 Pay inequalities

Pay inequalities have increased continually since 1990, as the pay of those in the top 10 per cent – both men and women – has risen faster than those at either the average or the bottom.

Half of part-time workers – both men and women – are paid less than £6.50 an hour. This compares with one in five full-time women and one in eight full-time men.

Disadvantaged at work

Choice of indicators

The two indicators for this theme address four different aspects of disadvantage at work.

The first indicator addresses jobs that are in some respect unsatisfactory. The first graph shows the number of people making a new claim for Jobseeker's Allowance – the benefit for people who are unemployed – within six months of last claiming. It is therefore, in effect, a measure of the extent to which the unemployed take jobs that turn out to be short-term ones only. The second graph develops this idea by showing, separately for people in part-time jobs and people in temporary employment, the extent to which people are in these jobs because they cannot find other ones.

The first graph of the second indicator shows the proportion of people aged 25 to retirement in work who have recently received work-related training in each of the last 10 years, these proportions being shown separately for people with and without qualifications. The second graph, on a quite different subject, shows how the proportion of employees belonging to a trade union varies according to their hourly rate of pay.

What the indicators show

Indicator 33 Insecure at work

Almost half of the men and a third of the women making a new claim for Jobseekers' Allowance were last claiming less than six months ago. These proportions are similar to a decade ago.

Only 10 per cent of part-time employees want a full-time job – but 30 per cent of temporary employees would like a permanent job.

Indicator 34 Support at work

Although there has been some improvement over the last decade, people with no qualifications are still three times less likely to receive job-related training than those with some qualifications.

15 per cent of workers earning less than £6.50 an hour belong to a trade union compared with 40 per cent of those earning £9 to £21 an hour.

Health and well-being

Choice of indicators

The first indicator relates to mortality. The first graph shows the proportion of both men and women aged under 65 who have died in each of the last 10 years. The supporting graph, again for men and women separately, shows the rates of deaths for the principal causes, namely heart disease and lung cancer, by social class.

The second indicator relates to morbidity. The first graph shows the proportion of people aged 45 to 64 who reported a long-standing illness or disability which limited their activity over the last decade, separately for men and women. The supporting graph provides a further breakdown by level of household income.

The final indicator concerns mental health, an issue which is widely agreed to be an important factor in poverty and social exclusion but for which the availability of tangible data is limited. The first graph shows how the proportion of people aged 25 to retirement who are judged to be at high risk of developing a mental illness has changed over the last decade, with the data shown separately for men and women. The second graph provides a further breakdown by level of household income.

What the indicators show

Indicator 35 Premature death

The rate of premature death fell by a sixth in the decade to 2004. It is, however, still one-and-a-half times as high among men as among women.

Death rates from heart disease and lung cancer – the two biggest causes of premature death – for people aged 35 to 64 are around twice as high among those from manual backgrounds as from non-manual backgrounds.

Indicator 36 Limiting long-standing illness

A quarter of adults aged 45–64 suffer a long-standing illness or disability which limits their activity.

Two-fifths of all adults in the poorest fifth of the population aged 45–64 have a limiting long-standing illness or disability, almost twice the rate for those on average incomes.

Indicator 37 Mental health

The proportion of adults aged 25 to retirement who are at a high risk of developing a mental illness is somewhat lower than a decade ago. Women are more at risk than men.

Adults in the poorest fifth are twice as likely to be at risk of developing a mental illness as those on average incomes.

Low income and work

23A: An adult's risk of low income varies greatly depending on how much paid work the household does. These risks have increased somewhat for all household types since the mid-1990s.

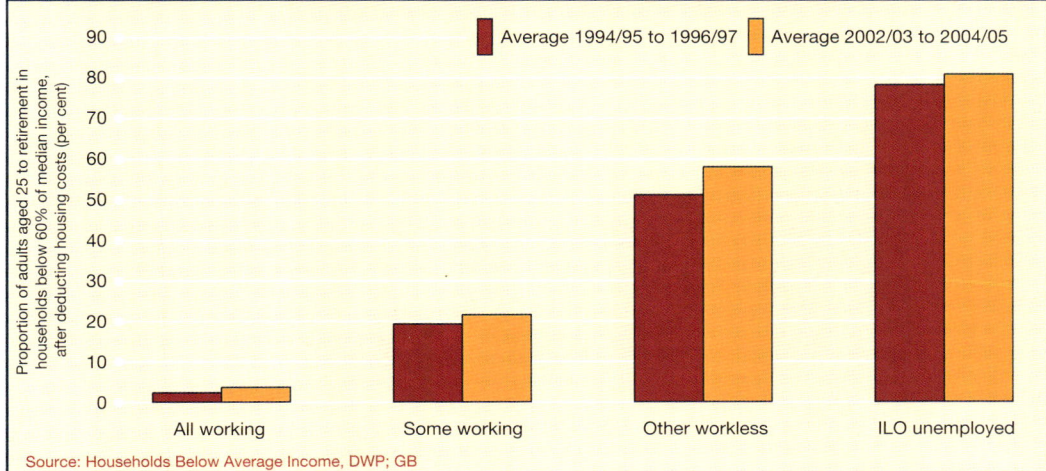

Legend: ■ Average 1994/95 to 1996/97 ■ Average 2002/03 to 2004/05

Y-axis: Proportion of adults aged 25 to retirement in households below 60% of median income, after deducting housing costs (per cent)

X-axis categories: All working, Some working, Other workless, ILO unemployed

Source: Households Below Average Income, DWP; GB

23B: Among those age 25 to retirement in low income households, the number who are in working households has been rising whilst the number who are in workless ones has been falling.

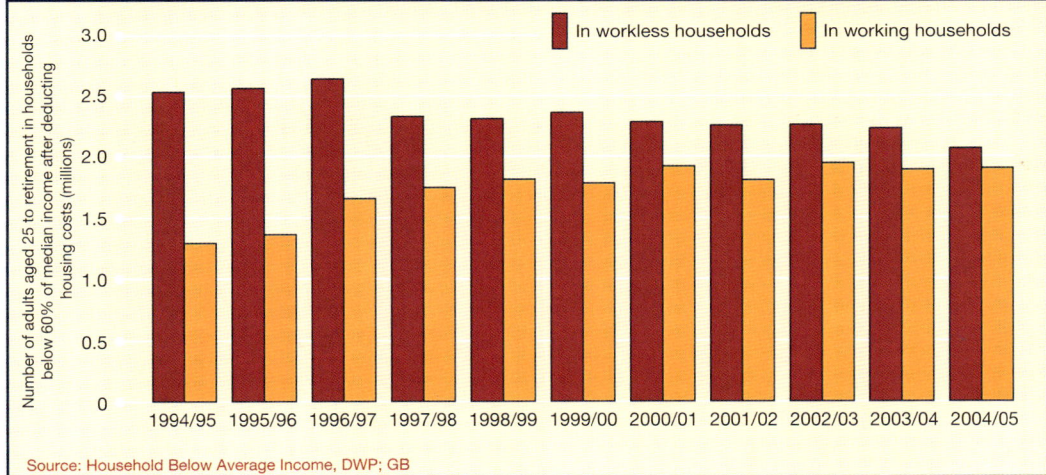

Legend: ■ In workless households ■ In working households

Y-axis: Number of adults aged 25 to retirement in households below 60% of median income after deducting housing costs (millions)

X-axis years: 1994/95, 1995/96, 1996/97, 1997/98, 1998/99, 1999/00, 2000/01, 2001/02, 2002/03, 2003/04, 2004/05

Source: Household Below Average Income, DWP; GB

The first graph shows the risk of an adult aged 25 to retirement being in a household below 60 per cent of median income after deducting housing costs, with the data shown separately for the following household work statuses: all working (single or couple, with one in full-time work and the other – if applicable – in full-time or part-time work); some working (includes households where no one is working full-time but one or more are working part-time); unemployed (head or spouse unemployed) and other workless (includes long-term sick/disabled and lone parents).

The second graph shows, over time, the number of adults aged 25 to retirement who are in low income households, with the data shown separately for households where someone is in paid work and for workless households.

The data source for both graphs is Households Below Average Income, based on the Family Resources Survey (FRS). The data relates to Great Britain and the self-employed have been excluded from the analysis. Income is disposable household income after deducting housing costs. All data is equivalised (adjusted) to account for variation in household size and composition.

Overall adequacy of the indicator: high. The FRS is a well-established annual government survey, designed to be representative of the population as a whole.

Low income and disability

24A: Disabled adults are twice as likely to live in low income households as non-disabled adults, and the gap has grown over the last decade.

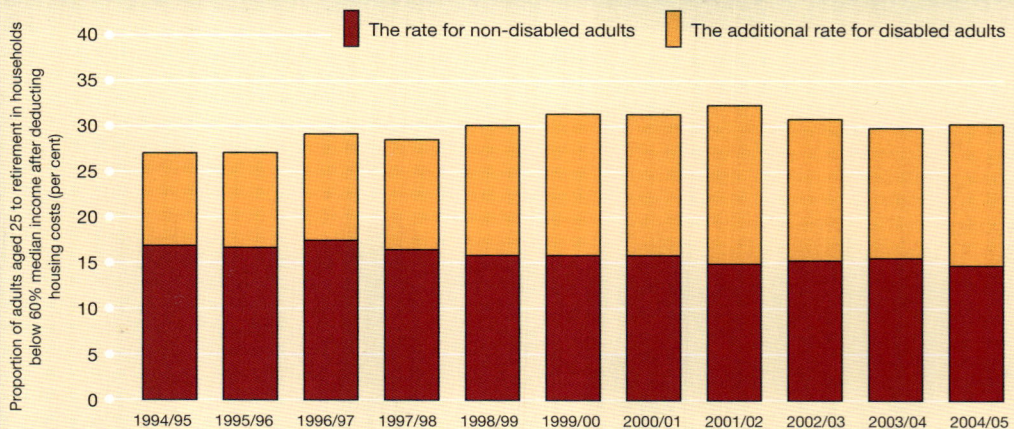

Legend:
- The rate for non-disabled adults
- The additional rate for disabled adults

Y-axis: Proportion of adults aged 25 to retirement in households below 60% median income after deducting housing costs (per cent)

X-axis years: 1994/95, 1995/96, 1996/97, 1997/98, 1998/99, 1999/00, 2000/01, 2001/02, 2002/03, 2003/04, 2004/05

Source: Households Below Average Income, DWP; GB

24B: Disabled people in workless households are somewhat less likely to be in low income than their non-disabled counterparts.

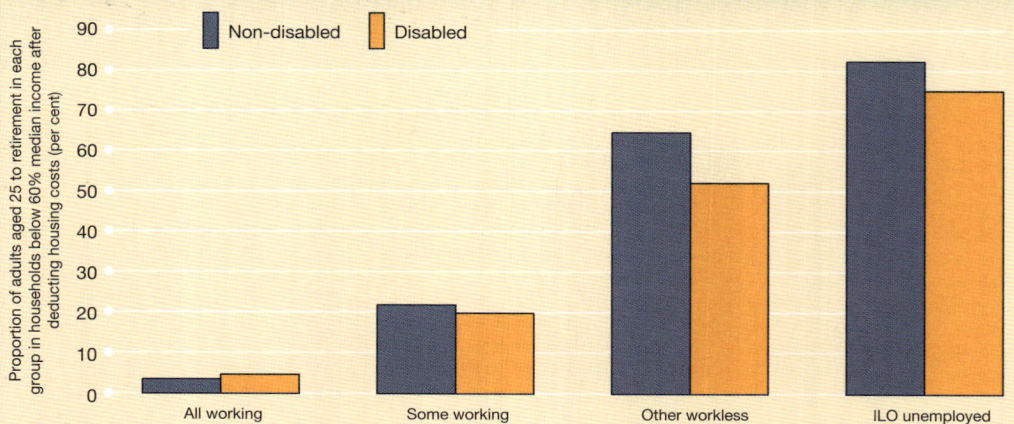

Legend:
- Non-disabled
- Disabled

Y-axis: Proportion of adults aged 25 to retirement in each group in households below 60% median income after deducting housing costs (per cent)

X-axis categories: All working, Some working, Other workless, ILO unemployed

Source: Households Below Average Income, DWP ; the data is the average for the years 2002/03 to 2004/05; GB

The first graph shows the proportion of adults aged 25 to retirement living in households below 60 per cent of median income after deducting housing costs, with the data shown separately for disabled and non-disabled adults.

The second graph shows how the risks of being in low income vary by work status, with the data shown separately for disabled and non-disabled working-age adults aged 25 to retirement. The following work statuses are shown: all working (single or couple, with one in full-time work and the other – if applicable – in full-time or part-time work); some working (includes households where no one is working full-time but one or more are working part-time); unemployed (head or spouse unemployed) and other workless (includes long-term sick/disabled and lone parents).

The data source for both graphs is Households Below Average Income, based on the Family Resources Survey (FRS). The data relates to Great Britain. Income is disposable household income after deducting housing costs. All data is equivalised (adjusted) to account for variation in household size and composition.

Overall adequacy of the indicator: high. The FRS is a well-established government survey, designed to be representative of the population as a whole.

Low income and Council Tax

25A: More than half of all low income households are paying full Council Tax, noticeably higher than in the mid-1990s.

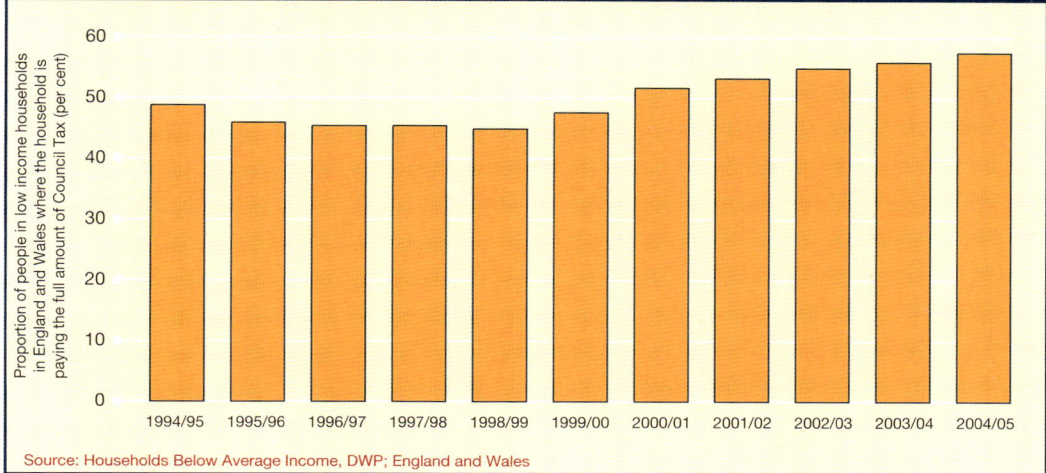

Source: Households Below Average Income, DWP; England and Wales

25B: 1½ million children in England and Wales are living in low income households where the household is paying full Council Tax.

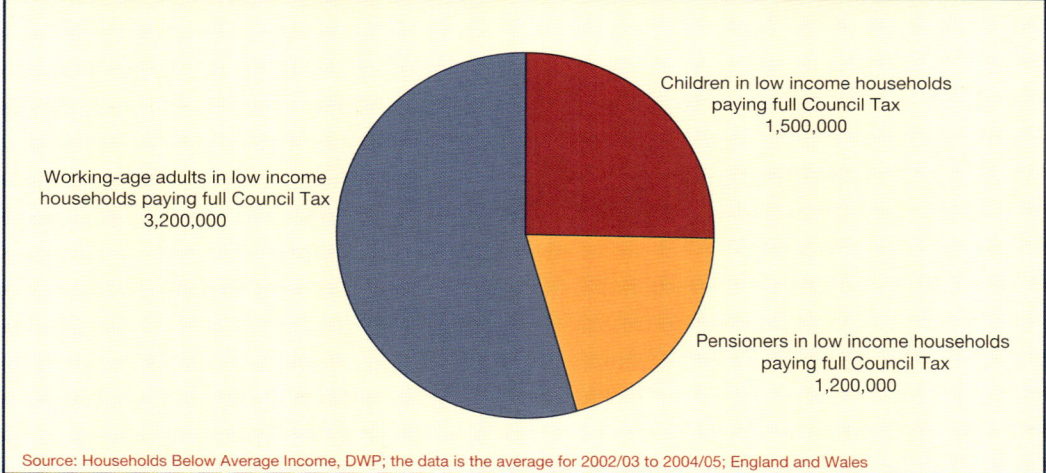

Children in low income households paying full Council Tax
1,500,000

Working-age adults in low income households paying full Council Tax
3,200,000

Pensioners in low income households paying full Council Tax
1,200,000

Source: Households Below Average Income, DWP; the data is the average for 2002/03 to 2004/05; England and Wales

The first graph shows, for each year, the proportion of people living in low income households where the household is paying the full amount of Council Tax (i.e. is not in receipt of any Council Tax Benefit).

The second graph shows, for selected household types for the latest year, the proportion of people living in low income households where the household is paying the full amount of Council Tax.

The data source for both graphs is Households Below Average Income, based on the Family Resources Survey (FRS). The data relates to England and Wales (in Scotland, Council Tax and water charges are paid as part of the same bill so it is not possible to distinguish people who are paying no Council Tax). Income is disposable household income after housing costs and is equivalised (adjusted) for household size and composition. The low income threshold is that used elsewhere, namely 60 per cent of median household income after deducting housing costs.

Overall adequacy of the indicator: medium. The FRS is a well-established annual government survey, designed to be representative of the population as a whole. However, the Council Tax data relates to a survey of what people were paying rather than to their actual bills.

Concentrations of low income

26A: 30% of working-age people receive out-of-work benefits in the areas with the highest concentrations. This compares with 10% in areas with average concentrations.

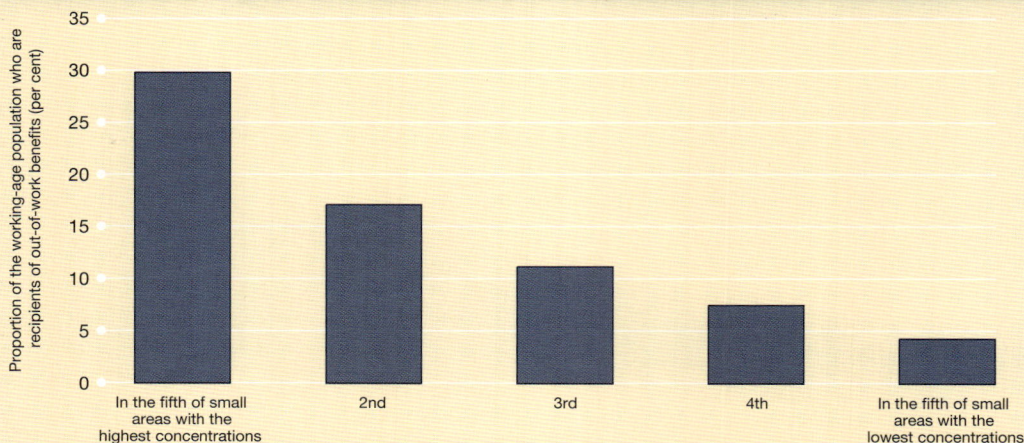

Proportion of the working-age population who are recipients of out-of-work benefits (per cent)

In the fifth of small areas with the highest concentrations	2nd	3rd	4th	In the fifth of small areas with the lowest concentrations

Source: DWP Work and Pensions Longitudinal Study; the data is for February 2006; GB

26B: Around 40% of working-age recipients of key out-of-work benefits live in a fifth of small areas, whilst the other 60% live outside of these areas.

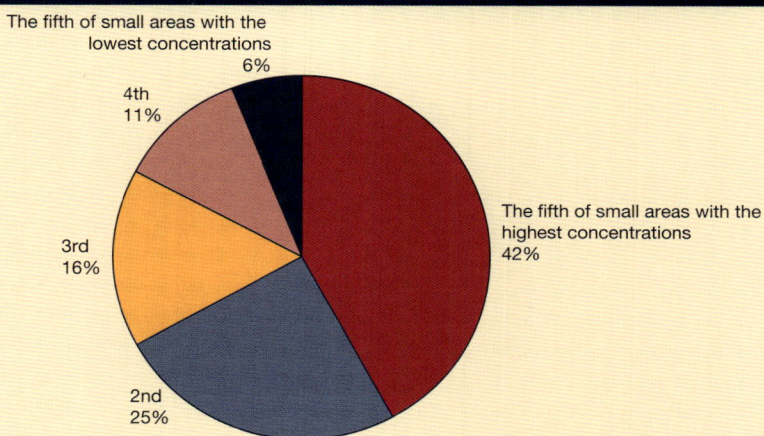

The fifth of small areas with the lowest concentrations 6%

4th 11%

3rd 16%

2nd 25%

The fifth of small areas with the highest concentrations 42%

Source: DWP Work and Pensions Longitudinal Study; the data is for February 2006; GB

This indicator examines how the pattern of recipiency of key out-of-work benefits by working-age people varies at a small area level. It does so by placing the 40,000 small areas ('super output areas') in Great Britain into five equal groups according to the proportion of their working-age population who are in receipt of such benefits. The benefits included are Jobseeker's Allowance, Income Support, Incapacity Benefit, Severe Disablement Allowance, and Carer's Allowance and, if someone is receiving more than one of these benefits, they are only counted once.

The first graph shows the extent to which rates of recipiency vary between the five groups and the second graph shows the proportion of the total recipients who are in each group. The data source is Department for Work and Pensions Work and Pensions Longitudinal Study and relates to Great Britain. The data is for February 2006.

Overall adequacy of the indicator: medium. The underlying data is a full count and is considered to be very reliable. But the data is a count of people in receipt of key out-of-work benefits rather than a count of people in low income. So, for example, it excludes all people in low pay and includes all recipients of out-of-work benefits even if they have some private income.

Wanting paid work

27A: Whereas the number officially unemployed has halved over the last decade, with particularly large falls in long-term unemployment, the number who are 'economically inactive' but want work has only fallen by a tenth.

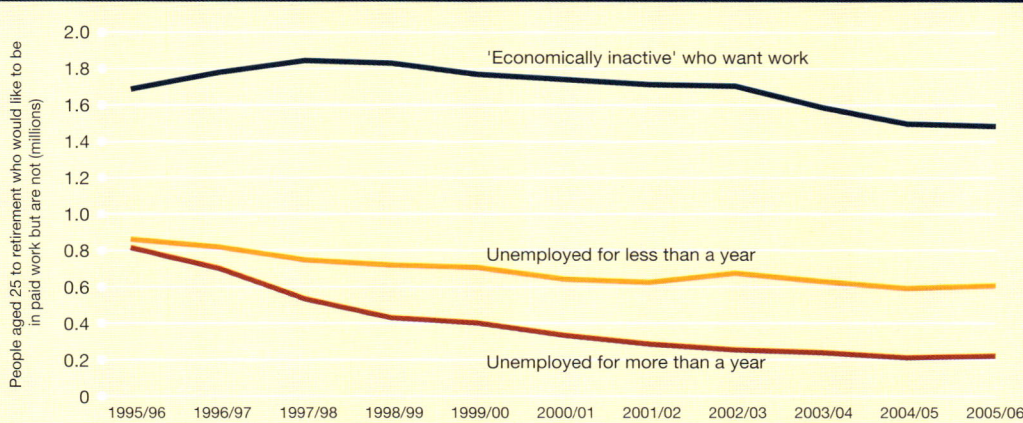

People aged 25 to retirement who would like to be in paid work but are not (millions)

'Economically inactive' who want work

Unemployed for less than a year

Unemployed for more than a year

1995/96 1996/97 1997/98 1998/99 1999/00 2000/01 2001/02 2002/03 2003/04 2004/05 2005/06

Source: Labour Force Survey, ONS; UK

27B: A third of those wanting paid work are unemployed. A further quarter are long-term sick or disabled.

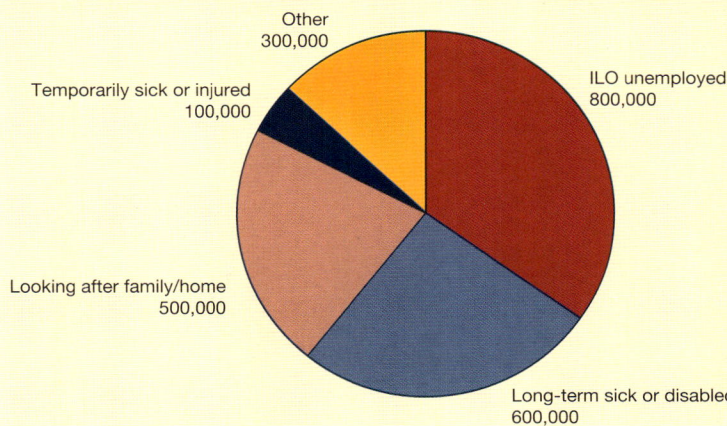

Other
300,000

Temporarily sick or injured
100,000

ILO unemployed
800,000

Looking after family/home
500,000

Long-term sick or disabled
600,000

Source: Labour Force Survey, ONS; the data is for the four quarters to winter 2005/06; UK

The first graph shows the number of people aged 25 to retirement wanting work. It is divided between the long-term unemployed, the short-term unemployed, and those counted as 'economically inactive' who nevertheless want paid work. 'Unemployment' is the ILO definition, which is used for the official UK unemployment numbers. It includes all those with no paid work in the survey week who were available to start work in the next fortnight and who either looked for work in the last month or were waiting to start a job already obtained. The economically inactive who want paid work includes people not available to start work for some time and those not actively seeking work. The data is based on a question in the Labour Force Survey asking the economically inactive whether they would like paid work or not.

The second graph shows, for the latest year, the proportions of those aged 25 to retirement who want paid work, by reason for their economic inactivity.

The data source for both graphs is the LFS. The data relates to the United Kingdom.

Overall adequacy of the indicator: high. The LFS is a well-established, quarterly government survey designed to be representative of the population as a whole.

Work and disadvantaged groups

28A: While the proportion of lone parents who are in paid work has increased a lot, the proportion of disabled people who are in paid work has only increased slightly.

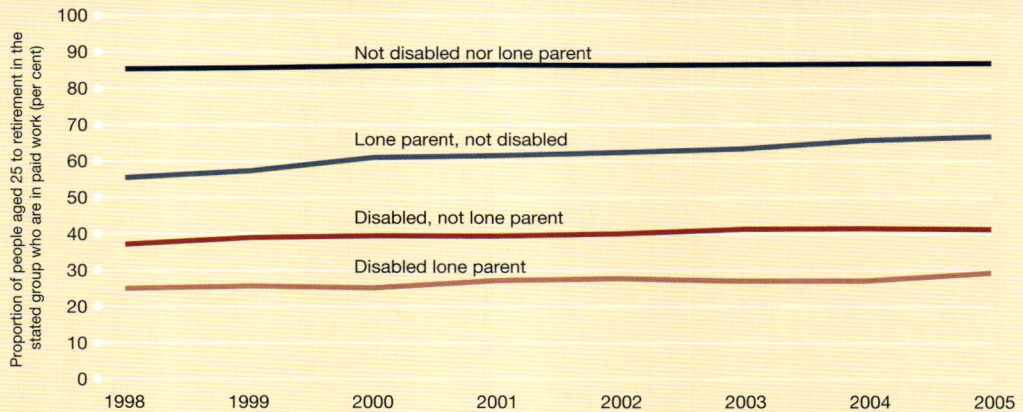

Proportion of people aged 25 to retirement in the stated group who are in paid work (per cent)

- Not disabled nor lone parent
- Lone parent, not disabled
- Disabled, not lone parent
- Disabled lone parent

1998 1999 2000 2001 2002 2003 2004 2005

Source: Labour Force Survey, ONS; UK

28B: At all levels of qualification, the proportion of people with a work-limiting disability who lack but want paid work is much greater than for those without a work-limiting disability.

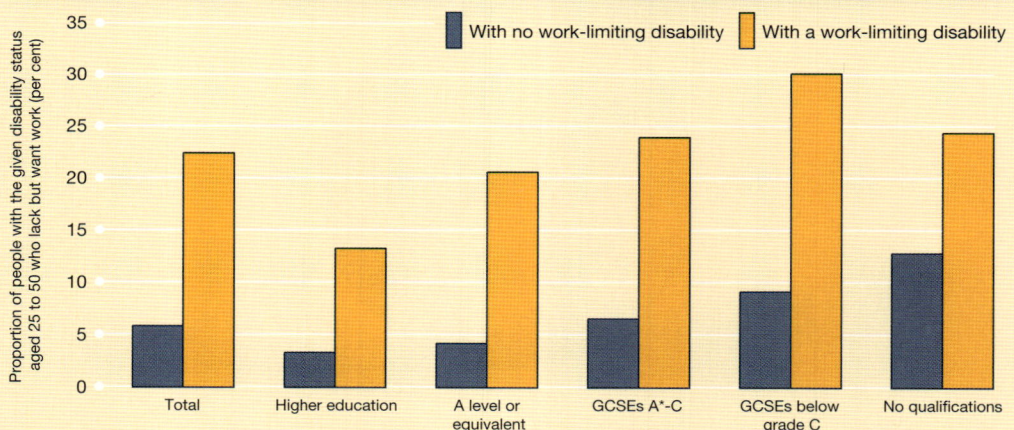

Proportion of people with the given disability status aged 25 to 50 who lack but want work (per cent)

■ With no work-limiting disability ■ With a work-limiting disability

Total | Higher education | A level or equivalent | GCSEs A*-C | GCSEs below grade C | No qualifications

Source: Labour Force Survey, ONS; the data is for the four quarters to winter 2005/06; UK

The first graph shows the proportion of people aged 25 to retirement who are in paid work, with the data shown separately for four groups of people, namely disabled lone parents, non-disabled lone parents, disabled people who are not lone parents, and people who are neither disabled nor lone parents. Disability is defined as those with a 'work-limiting disability' and comprises those people who stated that they have had health problems for more than a year and that these problems affect either the kind or amount of work they can do.

The second graph shows, for the latest year, how the proportion of people aged 25 to 50 who lack but want paid work (i.e. those who are ILO unemployed plus those who are economically inactive but want paid work) varies by level of disability and level of highest qualification.

The data source for both graphs is the Labour Force Survey (LFS) and relates to the United Kingdom. The data for each year is the average for the four quarters to the relevant winter.

Overall adequacy of the indicator: high. The LFS is a large, well-established, quarterly government survey, designed to be representative of the population as a whole.

Workless households

29A: While the number of 2+ adult working-age households who are workless has fallen, the number of single adult households who are workless has not.

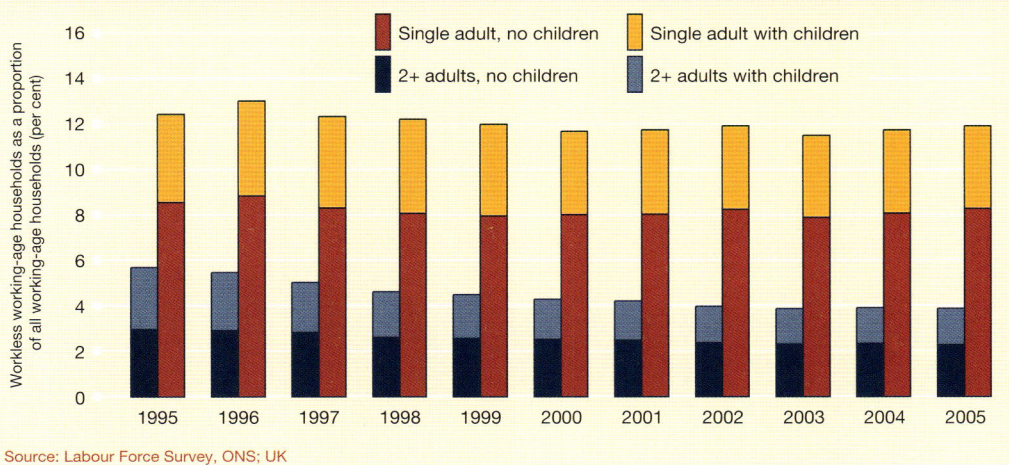

Legend:
- Single adult, no children
- Single adult with children
- 2+ adults, no children
- 2+ adults with children

Y-axis: Workless working-age households as a proportion of all working-age households (per cent)

X-axis years: 1995, 1996, 1997, 1998, 1999, 2000, 2001, 2002, 2003, 2004, 2005

Source: Labour Force Survey, ONS; UK

29B: The UK has a higher proportion of its working-age population living in workless households than most other EU countries.

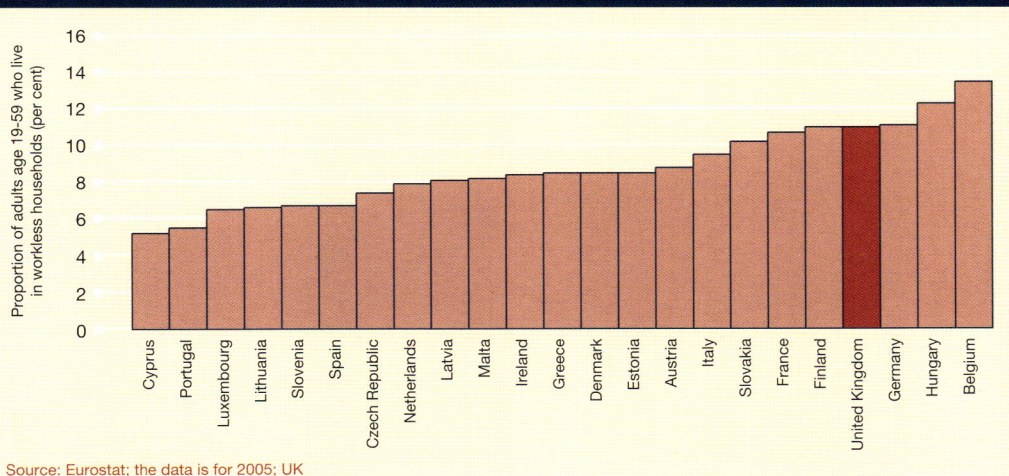

Y-axis: Proportion of adults age 19–59 who live in workless households (per cent)

X-axis countries: Cyprus, Portugal, Luxembourg, Lithuania, Slovenia, Spain, Czech Republic, Netherlands, Latvia, Malta, Ireland, Greece, Denmark, Estonia, Austria, Italy, Slovakia, France, Finland, United Kingdom, Germany, Hungary, Belgium

Source: Eurostat; the data is for 2005; UK

The first graph shows the number of workless working-age households (i.e. households where none of the adults are working) as a proportion of total working-age households, with the data being grouped into the following four household types: single adults without dependent children, lone parent households, households with two or more adults but no dependent children, and households with two or more adults and one or more dependent children. Households which are entirely composed of full-time students have been excluded from the analysis, as have households where their economic status is not known. Also, full-time students have been excluded from the calculations of whether or not the household has one or more than one adult. The data source is the Labour Force Survey (LFS) and the data for each year is the average for the spring and autumn quarters (analysis by household type not being available for the summer and winter quarters).

The second graph shows the proportion of adults aged 18 to 59 in each EU country who live in workless households. The data source is Eurostat, which in turn draws its data from the Labour Force Surveys in each country. The data is for the year 2005.

Overall adequacy of the indicator: high. The LFS is a large, well-established, quarterly government survey, designed to be representative of the population as a whole.

Low pay by gender

30A: The proportion of employees aged 22 and over who are low paid has fallen by around a fifth over the last five years. In 2005, 30% of the women – and 15% of the men – were paid less than £6.50 per hour.

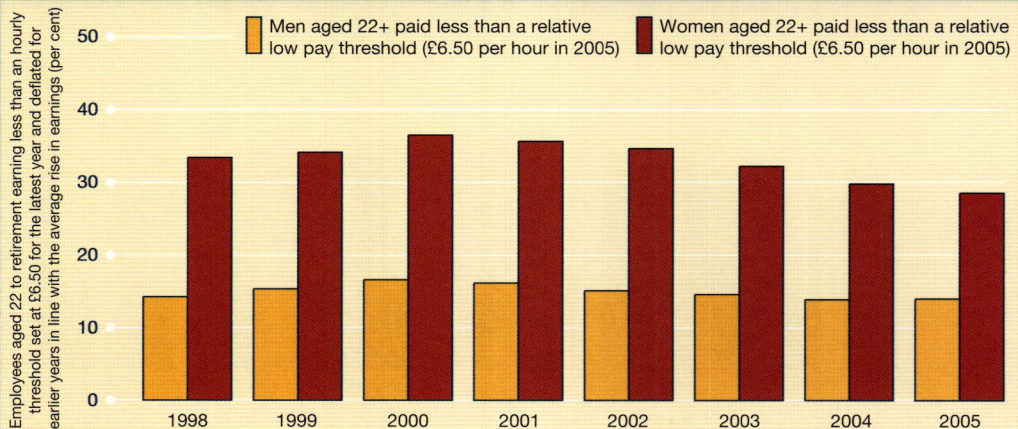

Men aged 22+ paid less than a relative low pay threshold (£6.50 per hour in 2005)

Women aged 22+ paid less than a relative low pay threshold (£6.50 per hour in 2005)

Employees aged 22 to retirement earning less than an hourly threshold set at £6.50 for the latest year and deflated for earlier years in line with the average rise in earnings (per cent)

Source: NPI calculations based on ONS estimates; UK

30B: Around half of those paid less than £6.50 per hour are part-time workers, mainly women.

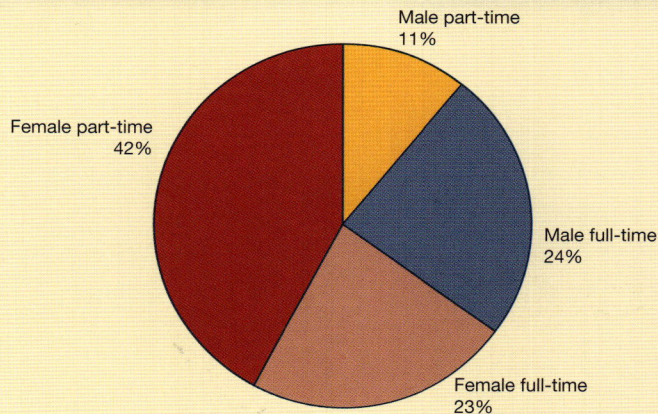

Male part-time 11%

Female part-time 42%

Male full-time 24%

Female full-time 23%

Source: Annual Survey of Hours and Earnings 2005, ONS; UK

The first graph shows the estimated proportion of employees aged 22 to retirement who were paid below an hourly pay threshold that rises in line with average earnings and reaches £6.50 in 2005. It is therefore £4.81 in 1998, £5.02 in 1999, £5.30 in 2000, £5.55 in 2001, £5.71 in 2002, £5.91 in 2003, £6.22 in 2004 and £6.50 in 2005. The data is shown separately for men and women. No data is available for years before 1998 and the available data only distinguishes between the 18-21 and 22+ age groups. The data is from published ONS statistics which were themselves derived from a combination of data from the Labour Force Survey (LFS) and Annual Survey of Hours and Earnings (ASHE), with adjustments by the ONS.

The second graph shows the distribution of employees paid less than £6.50 an hour by male/female and full-time/part-time. £6.50 an hour is roughly two-thirds of the Great Britain median hourly earnings and is commonly used as a threshold when analysing low pay. The data source is the ASHE.

Overall adequacy of the indicator: medium. The LFS and ASHE are well-established government surveys, designed to be representative of the population as a whole. However, the ONS methods for combining and adjusting the data are not available for public scrutiny, and the underlying dataset itself is not publicly available.

Low pay by industry

31A: Around half of employees aged 25 and over in the hotels & restaurants and wholesale & retail sectors earn less than £6.50 per hour. In both sectors, two-thirds of these people are women.

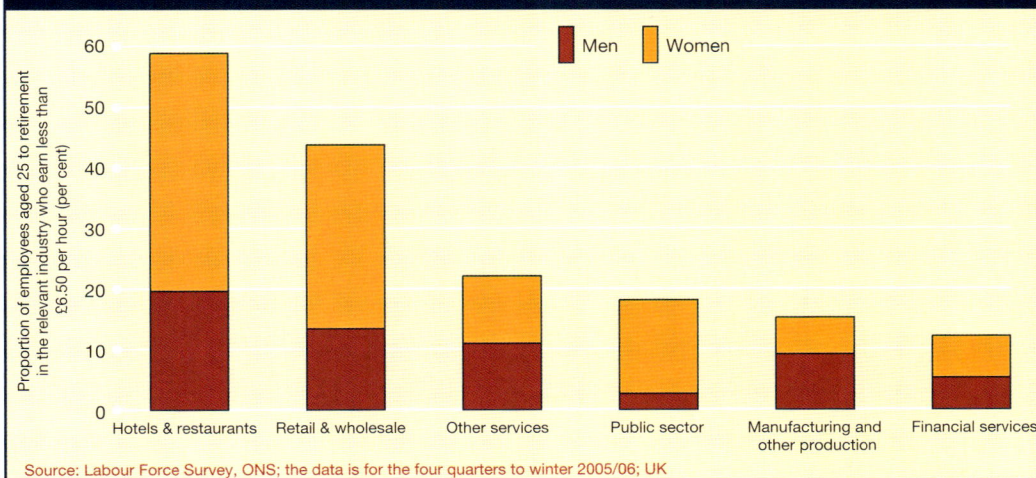

Source: Labour Force Survey, ONS; the data is for the four quarters to winter 2005/06; UK

31B: More than a quarter of all employees aged 25 to retirement earning less than £6.50 per hour work in the public sector.

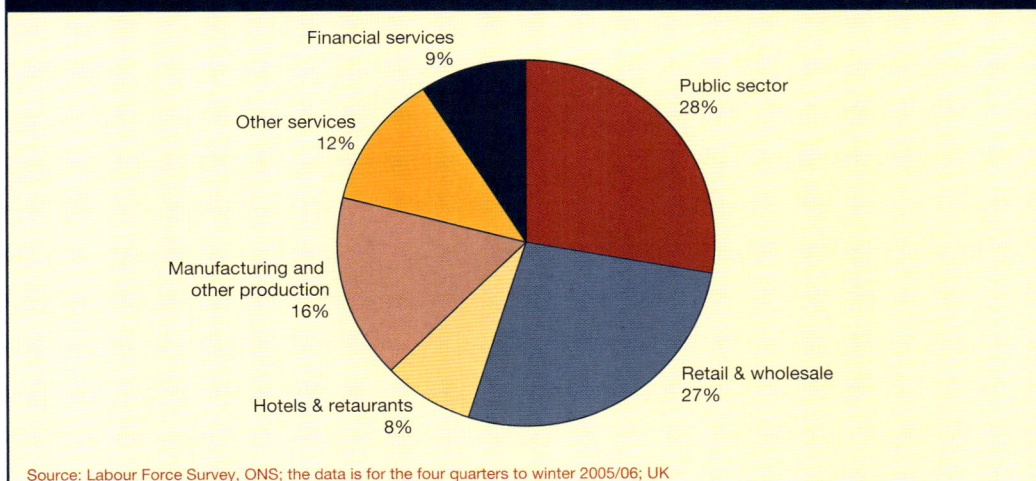

Source: Labour Force Survey, ONS; the data is for the four quarters to winter 2005/06; UK

The first graph shows how the proportion of workers aged 25 to retirement who were paid less than £6.50 an hour varies by industry sector, with the data shown separately for men and women.

The second graph shows the share of low paid workers aged 25 to retirement by industrial sector.

Some sectors have been combined for presentational purposes. The particular sectors shown are manufacturing and other production (section codes A-F); wholesale & retail (G); hotels & restaurants (H); public administration, education & health (L-N); other business activities (J-K); and other services (I & O-Q). A low pay threshold of £6.50 an hour has been used. This threshold is roughly two-thirds of the Great Britain median hourly earnings and is commonly used as a threshold when analysing low pay.

The data source for both graphs is the Labour Force Survey (equivalent data from the Annual Survey Hours and Earnings not being publicly available) and relates to the United Kingdom.

Overall adequacy of the indicator: medium. The Labour Force Survey is large, a well-established, quarterly government survey designed to be representative of the population as a whole but there are some doubts about the reliability of its low pay data.

Pay inequalities

32A: Pay inequalities have increased continually since 1990, as the pay of those in the top 10% – both men and women – has risen faster than those at either the average or the bottom.

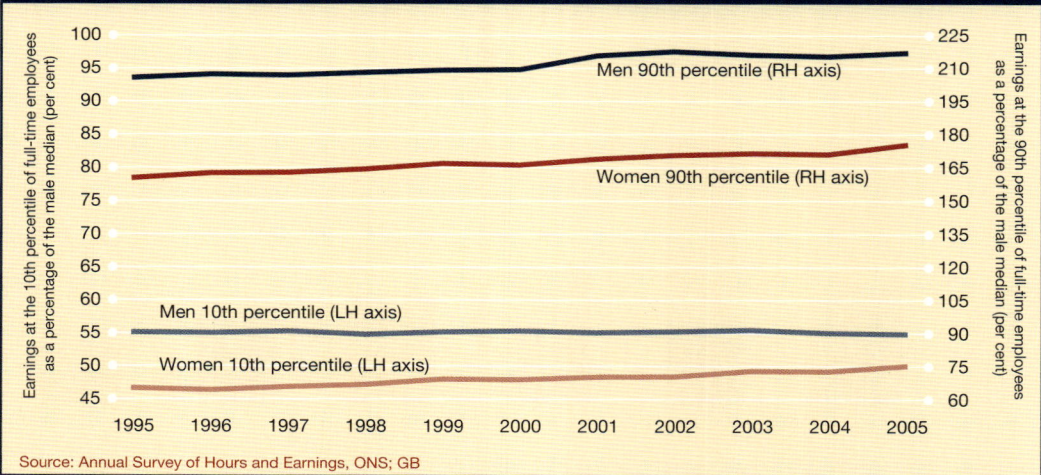

Earnings at the 10th percentile of full-time employees as a percentage of the male median (per cent)

Earnings at the 90th percentile of full-time employees as a percentage of the male median (per cent)

Men 90th percentile (RH axis)

Women 90th percentile (RH axis)

Men 10th percentile (LH axis)

Women 10th percentile (LH axis)

1995 1996 1997 1998 1999 2000 2001 2002 2003 2004 2005

Source: Annual Survey of Hours and Earnings, ONS; GB

32B: Half of part-time workers – both men and women – are paid less than £6.50 per hour. This compares with one in five full-time women and one in eight full-time men.

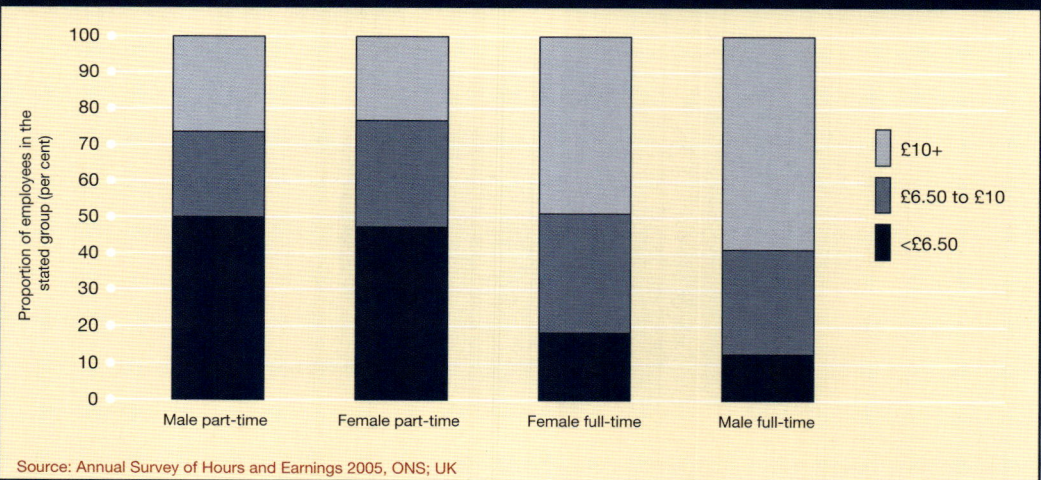

Proportion of employees in the stated group (per cent)

£10+

£6.50 to £10

<£6.50

Male part-time   Female part-time   Female full-time   Male full-time

Source: Annual Survey of Hours and Earnings 2005, ONS; UK

The first graph focuses on pay differentials. It shows gross hourly pay of full-time male and female employees at the 10th and 90th percentiles, i.e. the pay of men/women one tenth of the way from the bottom/top of the pay distribution for each gender. In each case, the statistics are shown as a proportion of average (median) hourly pay of full-time *male* employees thus providing a measure of earnings inequalities. The left-hand axis shows proportions at the 10th percentile and the right-hand axis shows the proportion at the 90th percentile. The data source is the New Earnings Survey (NES) up to 1998 and the Annual Survey of Hours and Earnings (ASHE) from 1998 onwards. The two surveys use slightly different methods of calculation so the NES figures have had a small adjustment applied to cater for this. Some detailed changes were made to the ASHE survey base in 2004 and an adjustment has also been made for this.

The second graph shows, for the latest year, the distribution of employees across the pay spectrum with the data shown separately for part-time women, part-time men, full-time women and full-time men. The data source is ASHE and the data relates to the United Kingdom.

Overall adequacy of the indicator: high. ASHE is a large annual survey of employers.

Insecure at work

33A: Almost half of the men, and a third of the women, making a new claim for Jobseeker's Allowance were last claiming less than six months ago. These proportions are similar to a decade ago.

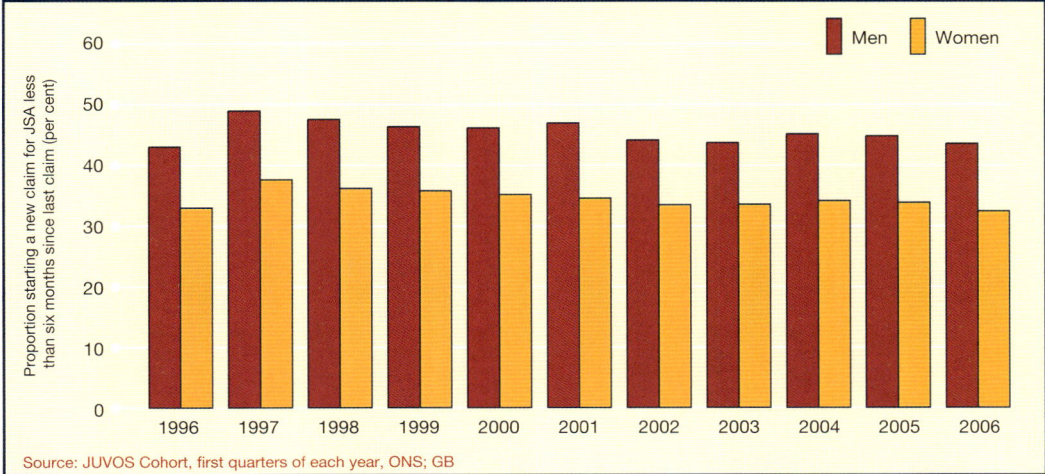

Proportion starting a new claim for JSA less than six months since last claim (per cent)

Men   Women

1996 1997 1998 1999 2000 2001 2002 2003 2004 2005 2006

Source: JUVOS Cohort, first quarters of each year, ONS; GB

33B: Only 10% of part-time employees want a full-time job – but 30% of temporary employees would like a permanent job.

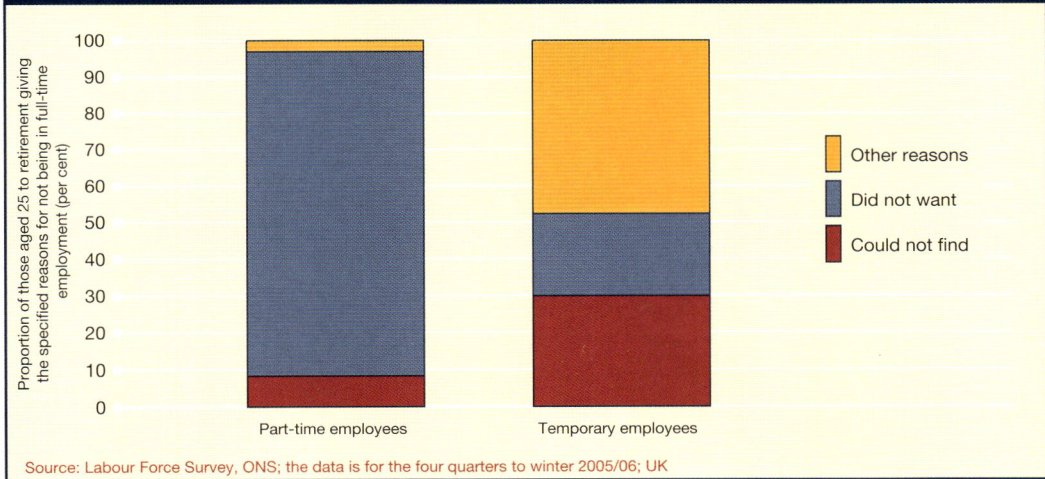

Proportion of those aged 25 to retirement giving the specified reasons for not being in full-time employment (per cent)

Other reasons

Did not want

Could not find

Part-time employees   Temporary employees

Source: Labour Force Survey, ONS; the data is for the four quarters to winter 2005/06; UK

The first graph tackles insecurity at work through the issue of people who find themselves taking a succession of jobs interspersed with periods of unemployment. It shows the probability that someone who makes a new claim for Jobseeker's Allowance was last claiming that benefit less than six months previously. This is effectively the same as the proportion of people finding work who then lose that work within six months. Figures are shown separately for men and women. The data relates to Great Britain and, for each year, is taken from the first quarter of the Joint Unemployment and Vacancies Operating System (JUVOS) cohort.

The second graph shows data for all employees aged 25 to retirement in part-time and temporary jobs (shown separately) by reason for the part-time or temporary employment. The data source is the Labour Force Survey (LFS) and relates to the United Kingdom.

Overall adequacy of the indicator: high. Note, however, that while the claimant count data is sound, the narrow definition of unemployment that it represents means that it understates the extent of short-term working interspersed with spells of joblessness.

Support at work

34A: Although there has been some improvement over the last decade, people with no qualifications are still three times less likely to receive job-related training than those with some qualifications.

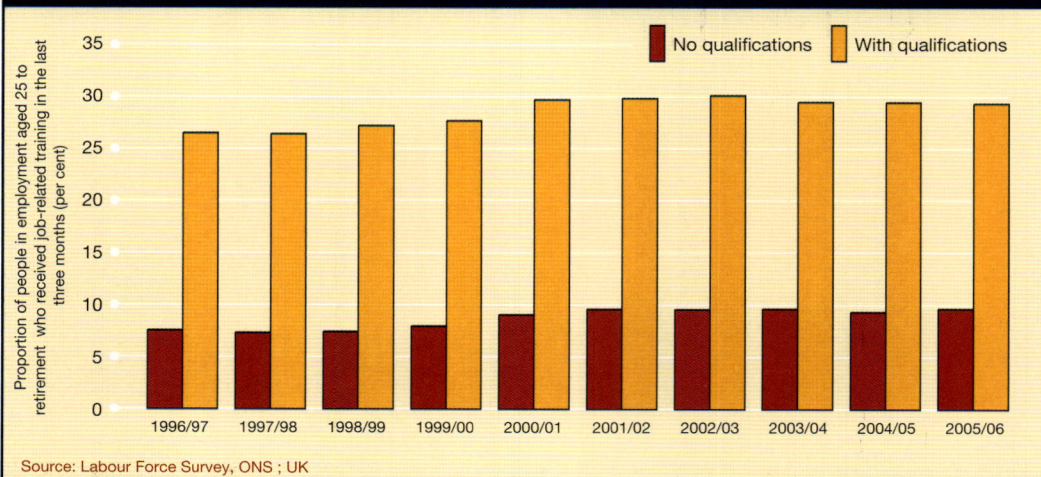

Proportion of people in employment aged 25 to retirement who received job-related training in the last three months (per cent)

■ No qualifications ■ With qualifications

35
30
25
20
15
10
5
0

1996/97 1997/98 1998/99 1999/00 2000/01 2001/02 2002/03 2003/04 2004/05 2005/06

Source: Labour Force Survey, ONS ; UK

34B: 15% of workers earning less than £6.50 an hour belong to a trade union compared with 40% of those earning £9 to £21 an hour.

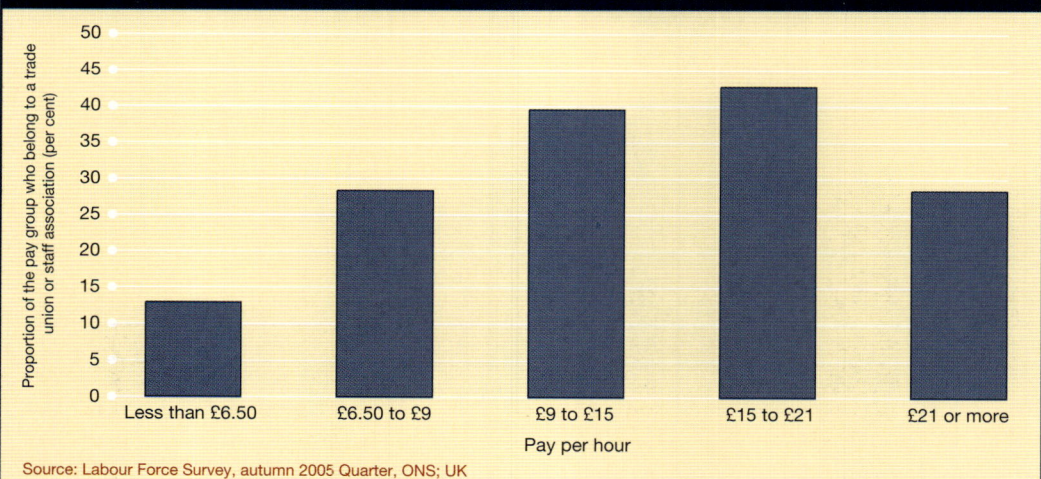

Proportion of the pay group who belong to a trade union or staff association (per cent)

50
45
40
35
30
25
20
15
10
5
0

Less than £6.50   £6.50 to £9   £9 to £15   £15 to £21   £21 or more

Pay per hour

Source: Labour Force Survey, autumn 2005 Quarter, ONS; UK

The first graph shows the proportion of employees aged 25 to retirement age who have received some job-related training in the previous three months according to whether they have some educational or vocational qualification or not. The qualifications include both current qualifications (e.g. GCSEs) and qualifications which have been awarded in the past (e.g. O levels). The data source is the Labour Force Survey (LFS) and the data relates to the United Kingdom. The training includes that paid for by employers and by employees themselves, and the data is for people aged 16 to retirement. Those who have a highest qualification which is not classifiable in the LFS (around 5 per cent of the total) have not been shown on the graphs on the grounds that they are likely to be a very disparate group.

The second graph shows the proportion of people currently employed who are members of a trade union or staff association, with the data shown separately by level of pay. The data source is LFS and relates to the United Kingdom. The figures are for the 2005 autumn quarter of the Labour Force Survey (the data is only collected in the autumn quarters).

Overall adequacy of the indicator: medium. The LFS is a well-established, quarterly government survey, designed to be representative of the population as a whole. But a single, undifferentiated notion of 'training', without reference to its length or nature, lessens the value of the indicator.

Premature death

35A: The rate of premature death fell by a sixth in the decade to 2004. It is, however, still one and a half times as high among men as among women.

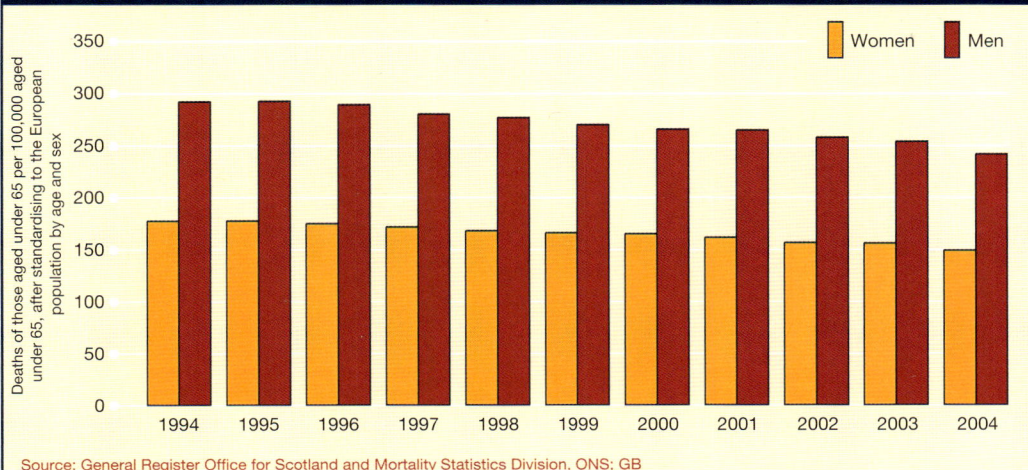

Legend: Women, Men

y-axis: Deaths of those aged under 65 per 100,000 aged under 65, after standardising to the European population by age and sex

x-axis: 1994, 1995, 1996, 1997, 1998, 1999, 2000, 2001, 2002, 2003, 2004

Source: General Register Office for Scotland and Mortality Statistics Division, ONS; GB

35B: Death rates from heart disease and lung cancer – the two biggest causes of premature death – for people aged 35 to 64 are around twice as high among those from manual backgrounds as from non-manual backgrounds.

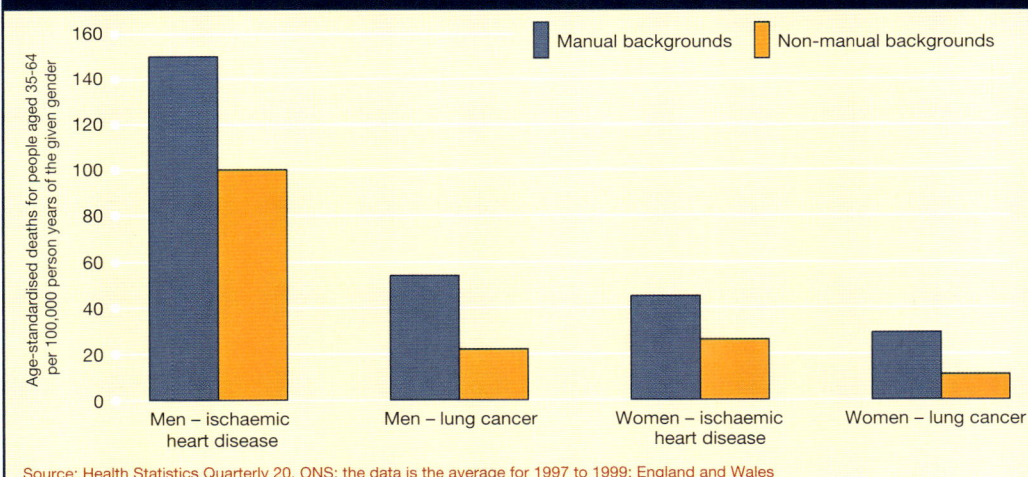

Legend: Manual backgrounds, Non-manual backgrounds

y-axis: Age-standardised deaths for people aged 35-64 per 100,000 person years of the given gender

x-axis: Men – ischaemic heart disease, Men – lung cancer, Women – ischaemic heart disease, Women – lung cancer

Source: Health Statistics Quarterly 20, ONS; the data is the average for 1997 to 1999; England and Wales

The first graph shows the number of deaths of people aged under 65 per 100,000 population aged under 65, with the data shown separately for males and females. The data source is the General Register Office (Scotland), Registrar General (Northern Ireland) and Mortality Statistics Division, ONS (England and Wales). The data relates to Great Britain. All data has been standardised to a constant European age structure. The data is actually published at local authority level and, to combine the local authority figures to calculate regional figures, the 2001 Census population estimates for the numbers of males and females under 65 have been used as the weighting factors.

The second graph compares death rates among those aged 35 to 64 by social class and gender for the two biggest causes of premature death, namely ischaemic heart disease and lung cancer. The data source is Health Statistics Quarterly 20 (Winter 2003), published by ONS. The data is the average for the years 1997 to 1999 and covers England and Wales. The data is the latest publicly available and the age group is the only one for which published data is available.

Overall adequacy of the indicator: high. The underlying data are deaths organised according to the local authority area of residence of the deceased by the ONS in England and Wales and by the Registrar General for Scotland.

Limiting long-standing illness

36A: A quarter of adults aged 45-64 suffer a long-standing illness or disability which limits their activity.

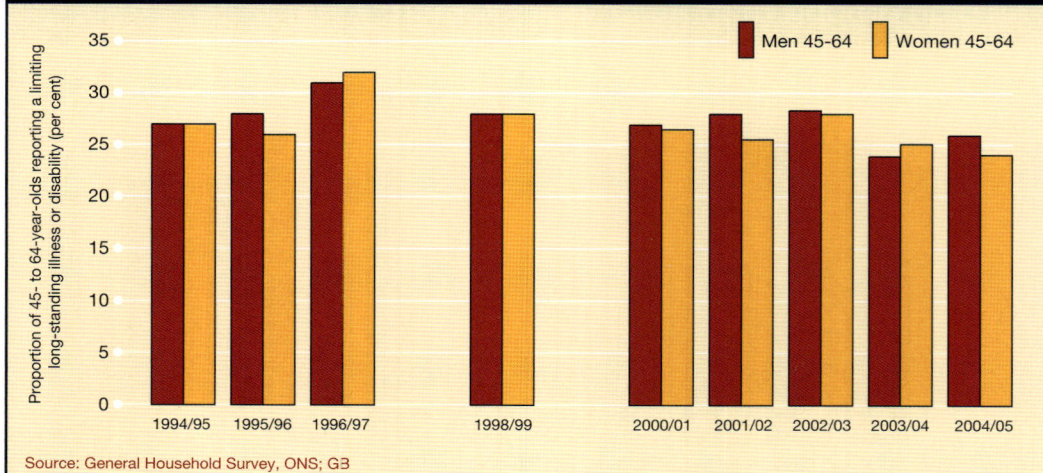

Men 45-64 · Women 45-64

Proportion of 45- to 64-year-olds reporting a limiting long-standing illness or disability (per cent)

1994/95 · 1995/96 · 1996/97 · 1998/99 · 2000/01 · 2001/02 · 2002/03 · 2003/04 · 2004/05

Source: General Household Survey, ONS; GB

36B: Two-fifths of all adults in the poorest fifth of the population aged 45-64 have a limiting long-standing illness or disability, almost twice the rate for those on average incomes.

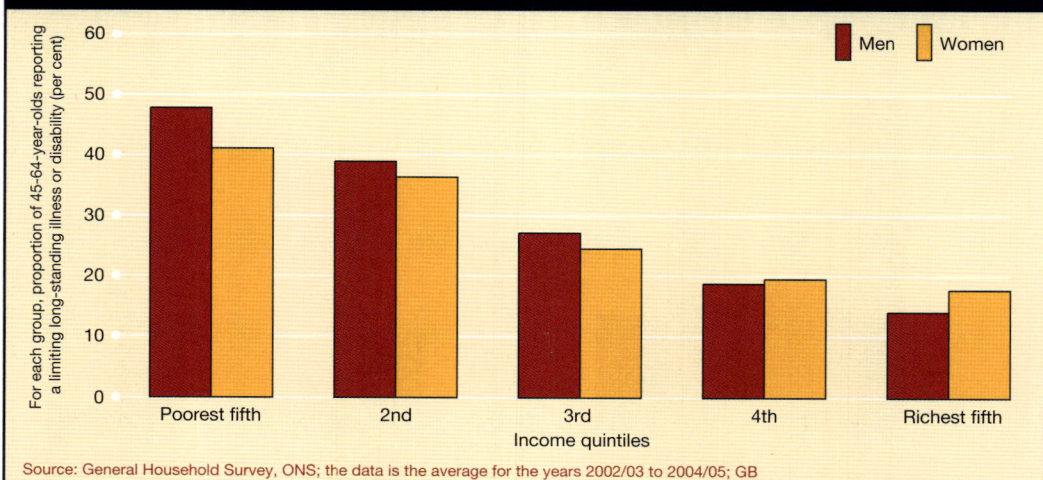

Men · Women

For each group, proportion of 45-64-year-olds reporting a limiting long-standing illness or disability (per cent)

Poorest fifth · 2nd · 3rd · 4th · Richest fifth

Income quintiles

Source: General Household Survey, ONS; the data is the average for the years 2002/03 to 2004/05; GB

The first graph shows the proportion of adults aged 45 to 64 who report having a long-term illness or a disability that limits the activities they are able to carry out. The data is shown separately for men and women.

The second graph shows how the proportions vary by income. Again, the data is shown separately for men and women. To improve its statistical reliability, the data is the average for the latest three years.

The data source for both graphs is the General Household Survey (GHS) and relates to Great Britain. The question asked was: 'Do you have any long-standing illness, disability or infirmity? Long-standing is anything that has troubled you over a period of time or that is likely to affect you over a period of time. Does this illness or disability limit your activities in any way?' Note that the data for 1997 and 1999 is missing because the GHS was not carried out in those years.

Overall adequacy of the indicator: medium. While the GHS is a well-established government survey designed to be representative of the population as a whole, the inevitable variation in what respondents understand and interpret as 'long-standing' and 'limiting activity', diminishes the value of the indicator.

Mental health

37A: The proportion of adults aged 25 to retirement who are at a high risk of developing a mental illness is somewhat lower than a decade ago. Women are more at risk than men.

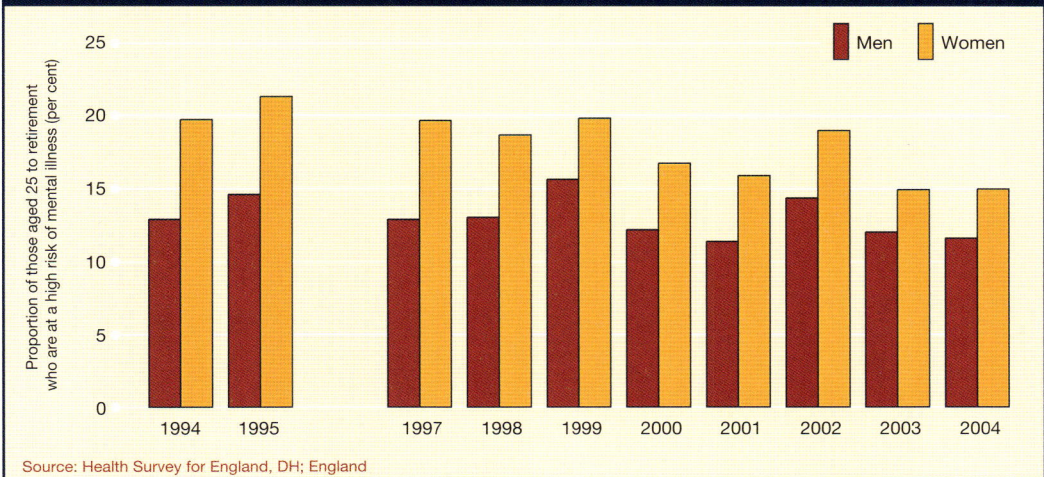

Source: Health Survey for England, DH; England

37B: Adults in the poorest fifth are twice as likely to be at risk of developing a mental illness as those on average incomes.

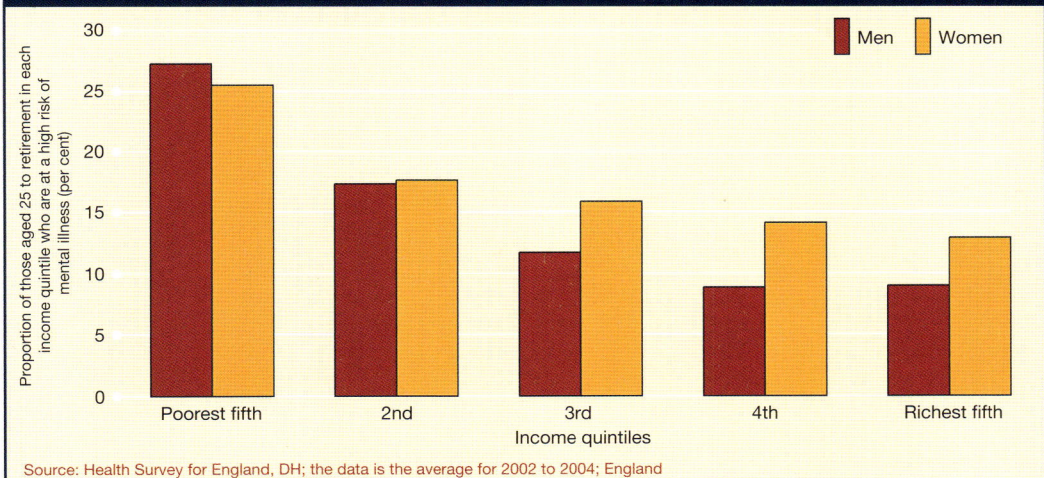

Source: Health Survey for England, DH; the data is the average for 2002 to 2004; England

The first graph shows the proportion of adults aged 25 to retirement who are classified as being at high risk of developing a mental illness, with the data shown separately for men and women. A high risk of mental illness is determined by asking informants a number of questions about general levels of happiness, depression, anxiety and sleep disturbance over the previous four weeks, which are designed to detect possible psychiatric morbidity. A score is constructed from the responses, and the figures published show those with a score of four or more. This is referred to as a 'high GHQ12 score'.

The second graph shows how the proportions vary by income, with the data shown separately for men and women.

The data source for both graphs is the Health Survey for England (HSE) and relates to England only. To improve statistical reliability, the data in the second graph has been averaged over the latest three years.

Overall adequacy of the indicator: medium. Whilst the HSE is a large survey designed to be representative of the population in England as a whole.

Chapter 5
Older people

Older people

This chapter has three themes containing six indicators in total. The themes are:

- economic circumstances;
- health and well-being;
- isolation and support.

Economic circumstances

Choice of indicators

The first indicator provides information on the degree to which different groups of pensioners have low incomes. The first graph shows these proportions for single pensioners and pensioner couples separately over the last decade. The supporting graph provides a further breakdown by gender and age.

The second indicator shows the proportion of pensioners who are entitled to, but not claiming key means-tested benefits, namely Pension Credit, Housing Benefit and Council Tax Benefit. The first graph shows these proportions annually over the last decade while the second reports them separately by tenure.

What the indicators show

Indicator 38 In low income households

Most of the fall in the proportion of pensioners in low income households has been among single pensioners rather than pensioner couples.

Older pensioner couples are much more likely to be in low income than younger pensioner couples. The differences are less for single pensioners.

Indicator 39 Non-take-up of benefits

Around two-fifths of pensioner households entitled to Council Tax Benefit and Pension Credit are not claiming it.

The proportion of pensioner households entitled to, but not claiming, Pension Credit is much higher for owner-occupiers than for those in other tenures.

Health and well-being

Choice of indicators

The first indicator relates to mortality. The first graph shows the extra number of people aged 65 or over who die in the winter months compared with the rest of the year. The supporting graph shows the proportion of pensioners who live in energy inefficient housing, separately by tenure and level of income.

The second indicator relates to morbidity. The first graph shows the proportions reporting that they suffer from a limiting long-standing illness or disability, separately for those under and over age 75, annually over the last decade. The second graph, again comparing those under 75 with those over, shows these proportions by level of household income.

What the indicators show

Indicator 40 Excess winter deaths

Each year between 20,000 and 50,000 more people aged 65 or over die in winter months than in other months.

Among older people, it is private renters who are the most likely to live in energy inefficient housing, followed by owner occupiers on low incomes.

Indicator 41 Limiting long-standing illness

A third of adults aged 65–74, and almost half of adults aged 75 and over, report a limiting long-standing sickness or disability.

Adults aged 65–74 on below average incomes are more likely to have a limiting long-standing illness or disability than those on above average incomes. For those aged 75 and over, this has ceased to be the case.

Isolation and support

Choice of indicators

Isolation and support are important aspects of social exclusion for older people but the tangible data that is available for analysis is very limited.

The first indicator looks at the number of people aged 75 or over who receive home care from their local authority. The first graph shows the proportion helped year by year over the last decade, with a division in later years between those receiving intensive help and those receiving non-intensive help only. The supporting graph shows how the proportion varies for different types of local authorities, ranging from county councils to inner London boroughs.

The second indicator shows the proportion of people aged 60 or over who report feeling very unsafe out at night. The first graph shows these proportions separately for men and women over the last decade while the supporting graph shows how these proportions vary by level of household income.

What the indicators show

Indicator 42 Help to live at home

The proportion of older people receiving home care has almost halved since 1994 as available resources are increasingly focused on those deemed most in need.

On average, English county councils support fewer older people to live independently at home than either urban or Welsh authorities.

Indicator 43 Anxiety

Among those aged 60 or over, women are three times as likely to feel very unsafe out at night as men.

Among women aged 60 and over, those from lower income households are one-and-a-half times as likely to feel very unsafe out at night as those from higher income households.

In low income households

38A: Most of the fall in the proportion of pensioners in low income households has been among single pensioners rather than pensioner couples.

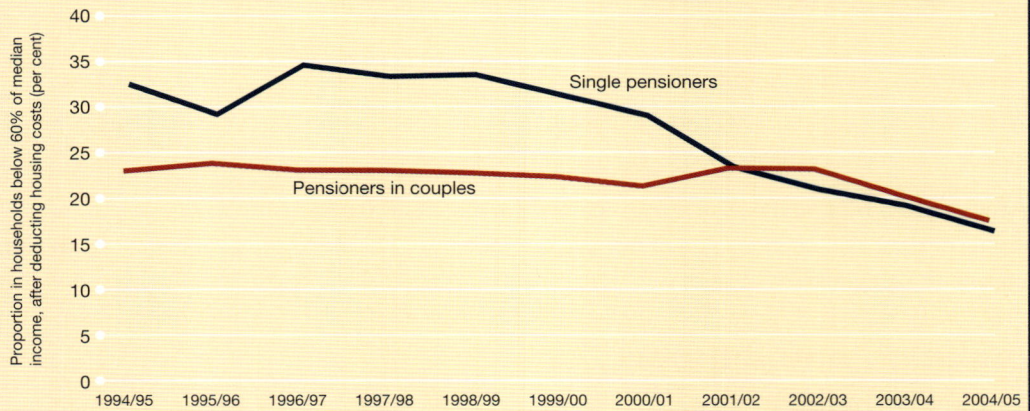

Proportion in households below 60% of median income, after deducting housing costs (per cent)

Single pensioners

Pensioners in couples

1994/95 1995/96 1996/97 1997/98 1998/99 1999/00 2000/01 2001/02 2002/03 2003/04 2004/05

Source: Households Below Average Income, DWP; GB

38B: Older pensioner couples are much more likely to be in low income than younger pensioner couples. The differences are less for single pensioners.

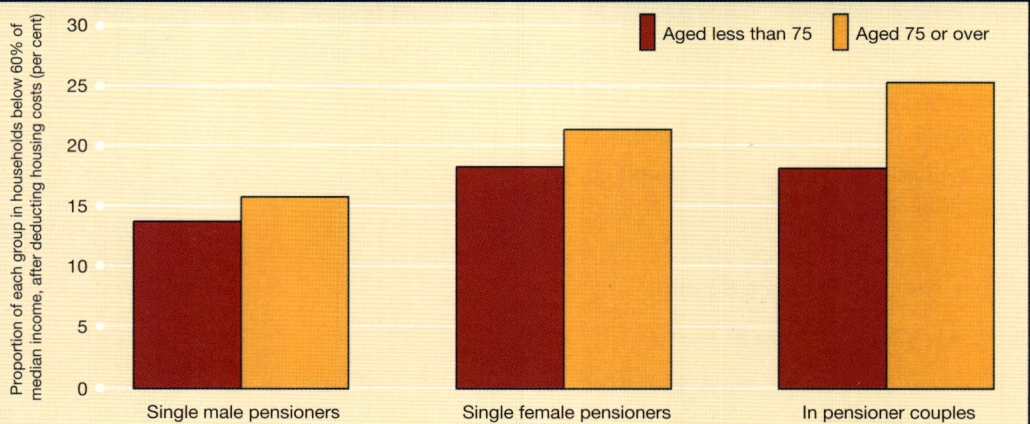

Proportion of each group in households below 60% of median income, after deducting housing costs (per cent)

Aged less than 75   Aged 75 or over

Single male pensioners   Single female pensioners   In pensioner couples

Source: Household Below Average Income, DWP; the data is the average for 2002/03 to 2004/05; GB

The first graph shows the risk of a pensioner being in a low income household (defined as the proportion of people with incomes below 60 per cent of median household income after deducting housing costs), with the data shown separately for single pensioners and pensioner couples.

The second graph shows the proportion of pensioners living in low income households for different combinations of age group and family type. To improve statistical reliability, the data is the average for the latest three years.

The data source for both graphs is Households Below Average Income, based on the Family Resources Survey (FRS). The data relates to Great Britain. Income is disposable household income after deducting housing costs. All data is equivalised (adjusted) to account for variation in household size and composition.

Overall adequacy of the indicator: high. The FRS is a well-established annual government survey designed to be representative of the population as a whole. However, since it only covers people living in private households, and not residential institutions (such as nursing homes), it does leave out a significant group of older people.

Non-take-up of benefits

39A: Around two-fifths of pensioner households entitled to Council Tax Benefit and Pension Credit are not claiming it.

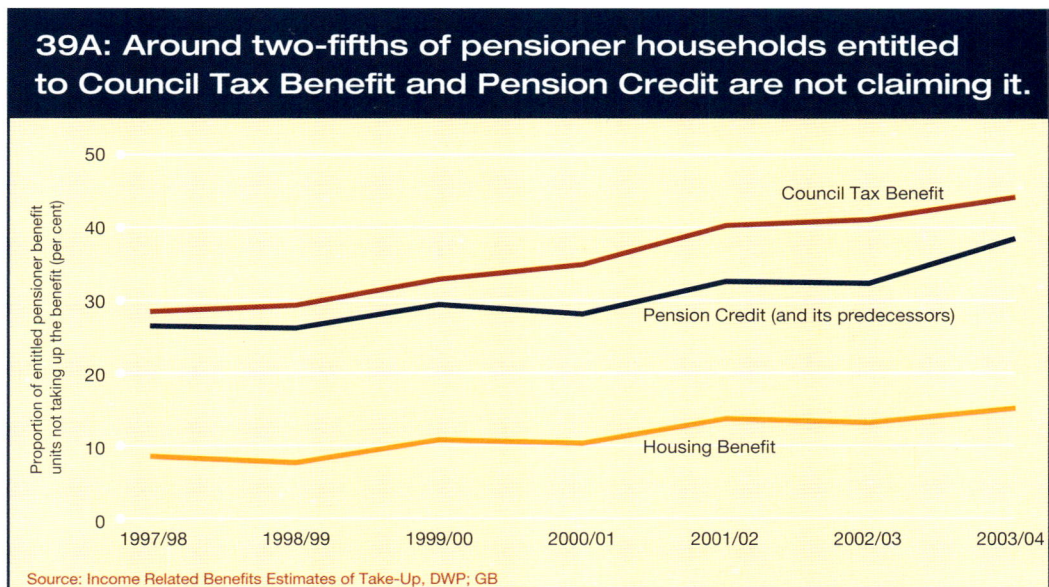

Source: Income Related Benefits Estimates of Take-Up, DWP; GB

39B: The proportion of pensioner households entitled to, but not claiming, Pension Credit is much higher for owner-occupiers than for those in other tenures.

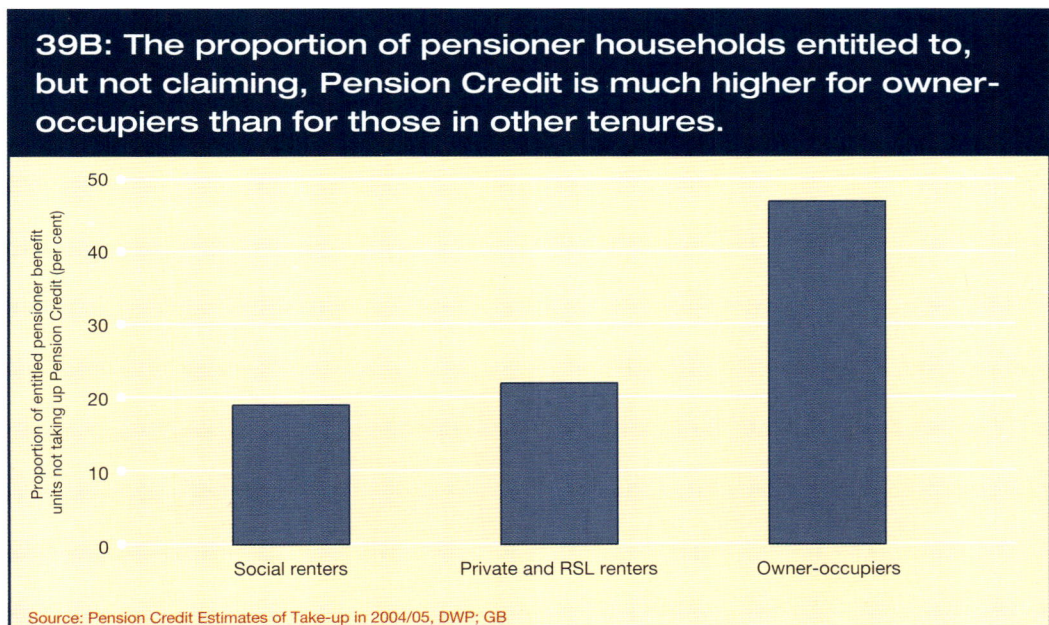

Source: Pension Credit Estimates of Take-up in 2004/05, DWP; GB

The first graph shows the estimated proportion of pensioner households entitled to selected benefits who are not taking up their entitlement. The benefits shown are the three major benefits of older people, namely Council Tax Benefit, Pension Credit (and its predecessors) and Housing Benefit. In each case, the estimates are the averages for low end and high end estimates published by DWP.

The second graph shows, for the latest year, the estimated proportion of pensioner households in each housing tenure who are entitled to Pension Credit but are not taking up their entitlement. Note that the data groups households renting from registered social landlords with private renters rather than with those renting from local authorities. Also note that data by tenure is not available for either Housing Benefit or Council Tax Benefit.

The data source for both graphs is the Income-related Benefits: Estimates of Take-up series published by the Department for Work and Pensions (DWP) and the data relates to Great Britain. Note that, in all the graphs, the figures shown are the mid-points of quite wide range estimates, so the figures for any particular benefit in any particular year are subject to considerable uncertainty.

Overall adequacy of the indicator: medium. The figures are estimates only, based on the modelling of data from surveys such as the Family Resources Survey.

Excess winter deaths

40A: Each year between 20,000 and 50,000 more people aged 65 or over die in winter months than in other months.

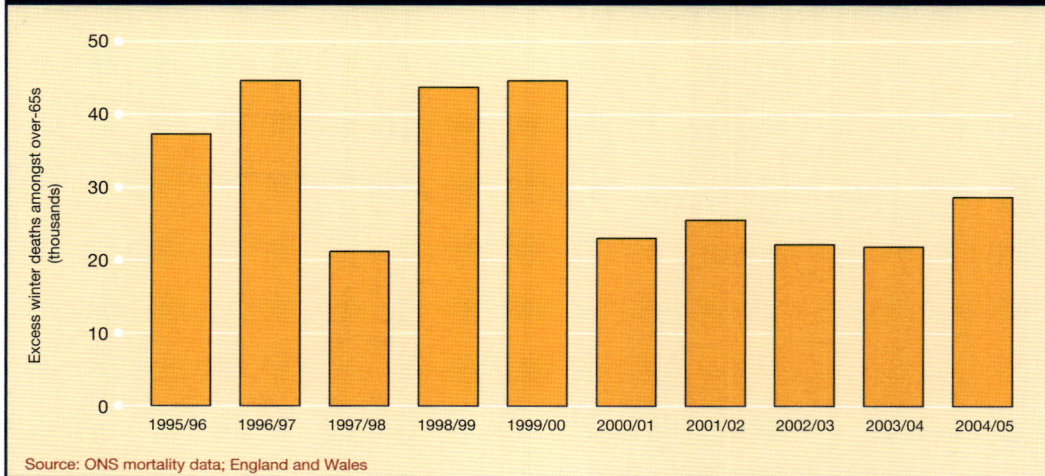

Excess winter deaths amongst over-65s (thousands)

1995/96	37
1996/97	45
1997/98	21
1998/99	44
1999/00	45
2000/01	23
2001/02	25
2002/03	22
2003/04	21
2004/05	29

Source: ONS mortality data; England and Wales

40B: Among older people, it is private renters who are the most likely to live in energy inefficient housing, followed by owner occupiers on low incomes.

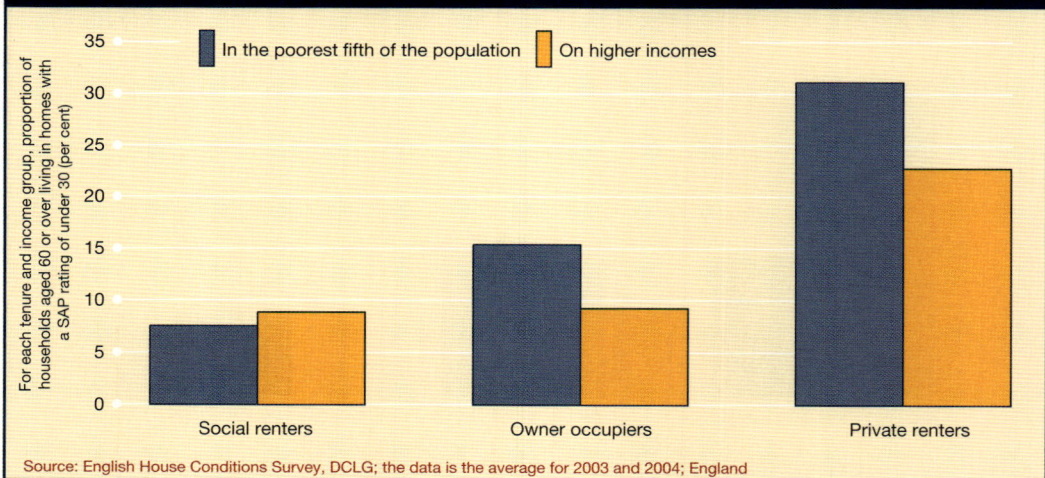

For each tenure and income group, proportion of households aged 60 or over living in homes with a SAP rating of under 30 (per cent)

- In the poorest fifth of the population
- On higher incomes

	Poorest fifth	Higher incomes
Social renters	7.5	8.5
Owner occupiers	15	9
Private renters	31	22.5

Source: English House Conditions Survey, DCLG; the data is the average for 2003 and 2004; England

The first graph shows excess winter deaths each year in the 65 and over age group, where 'excess winter deaths' is defined as the difference between the number of deaths which occurred in winter (December to March) and the average number of deaths during the preceding and subsequent four months. The data source is ONS mortality data and is for England and Wales.

The second graph shows the proportion of households aged 60 and over who live in homes with a Standard Assessment Procedure (SAP) rating of less than 30, with the data separated out by housing tenure and by level of household income. SAP ratings are a measure of energy efficiency (the higher the SAP rating, the better) ranging from 0 to 100. The threshold of 30 has been used following advice from the Department for Communities and Local Government (DCLG). The data source is the English House Conditions Survey and the data relates to England. To improve its statistical reliability, the data is the average for 2003 and 2004 (there was no survey in 2002).

Overall adequacy of the indicator: medium. Whilst the data sources used here are reliable ones, there is no data providing evidence of a direct causal relationship between winter deaths and energy inefficient housing.

Limiting long-standing illness

41A: A third of adults aged 65-74, and almost half of adults aged 75 and over, report a limiting long-standing sickness or disability.

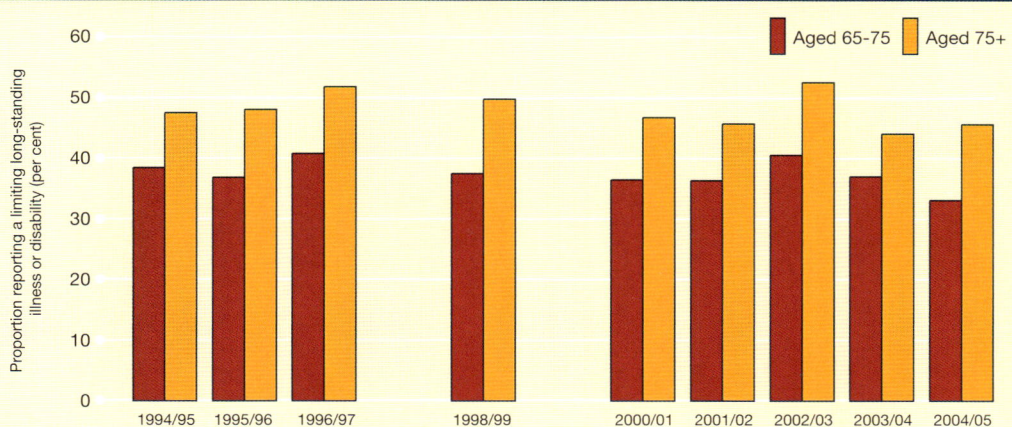

Source: General Household Survey, ONS; GB

41B: Adults aged 65-74 on below average incomes are more likely to have a limiting long-standing illness or disability than those on above average incomes. For those aged 75 and over, this has ceased to be the case.

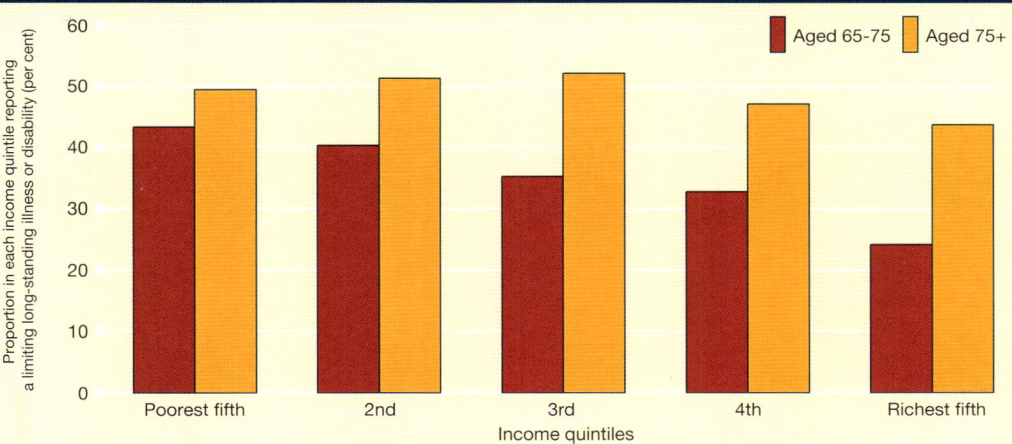

Source: General Household Survey, ONS; the data is the average for the years 2002/03 to 2004/05; GB

The first graph shows the proportion of people aged 65 and over who report having a long-standing illness or a disability that limits the activities they are able to carry out. The data is shown separately for those aged 65-74 and those aged 75+.

The second graph shows how the proportions vary by income. Again, the data is shown separately for those aged 65-74 and those aged 75+. To improve its statistical reliability, the data is the average for the latest three years.

The data for both graphs is from the General Household Survey (GHS) and relates to Great Britain. The question asked was: 'Do you have any long-standing illness, disability or infirmity? Long-standing is anything that has troubled you over a period of time or that is likely to affect you over a period of time. Does this illness or disability limit your activities in any way?' Note that the data for 1997 and 1999 is missing because the GHS was not carried out in those years.

Overall adequacy of the indicator: medium. While the GHS is a well-established government survey, the inevitable variation in what respondents understand and interpret as 'long-standing' and 'limiting activity', diminishes the value of the indicator.

Help to live at home

42A: The proportion of older people receiving home care has almost halved since 1994 as available resources are increasingly focused on those deemed most in need.

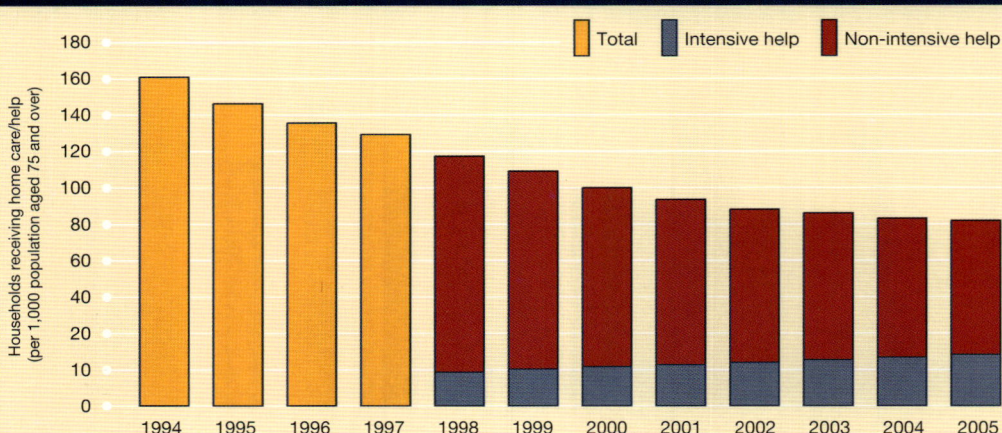

Legend: Total · Intensive help · Non-intensive help

Y-axis: Households receiving home care/help (per 1,000 population aged 75 and over)

X-axis: 1994, 1995, 1996, 1997, 1998, 1999, 2000, 2001, 2002, 2003, 2004, 2005

Source: Dept. of Health returns HH1 and ONS population estimates; England

42B: On average, English county councils support fewer older people to live independently at home than either urban or Welsh authorities.

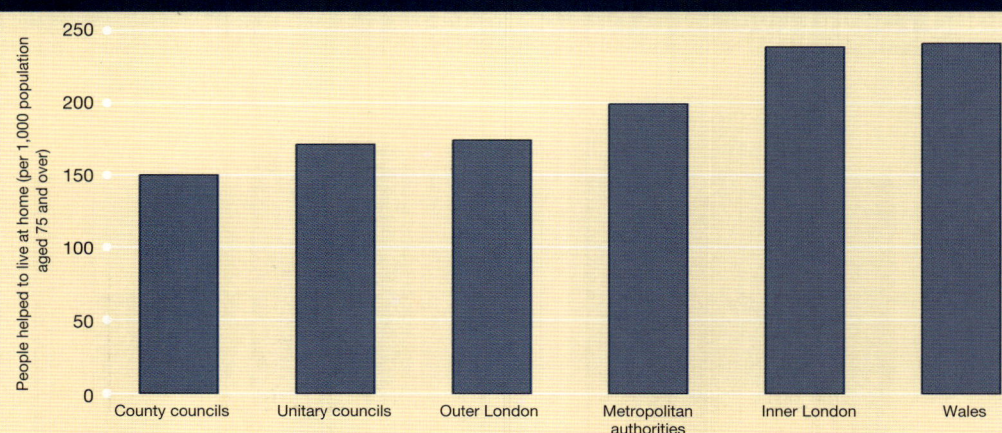

Y-axis: People helped to live at home (per 1,000 population aged 75 and over)

X-axis: County councils, Unitary councils, Outer London, Metropolitan authorities, Inner London, Wales

Source: Audit Commission Performance Indicators for England and Local Government Data Unit for Wales; the data is for 2004/05; England and Wales

The first graph shows the number of households receiving home help/care from their local authority. The data is expressed per 1,000 population aged 75 and over on the grounds that the majority of people receiving home help/care are in this age group. From 1998 onwards, the data is shown separately for those receiving intensive help (more than 10 hours a week or 6 or more visits) but this division is not available for the earlier years. 'Being helped to live at home' includes provision of: home help services; practical services which assist the client to function as independently as possible and/or continue to live in their own homes; and overnight, live-in and 24-hour services. The data source is the Department of Health HH1 returns and the data relates to England.

The second graph shows how the proportion of people being helped to live at home varies by type of authority. Note that 'being helped to live at home' is a wider measure than the 'receiving home help/care' in the first graph as it includes meals-on-wheels, day care etc. The data source is the Local Government Data Unit for Wales (Wales) and the Audit Commission Best Value Performance Indicators (England). The data is for 2004/05.

Overall adequacy of the indicator: medium. The underlying data has been collected for a number of years and can be considered reliable. However, comparisons have to be qualified because statistics ideally ought to be measured in relation to need.

Anxiety

43A: Among those aged 60 or over, women are three times as likely to feel very unsafe out at night as men.

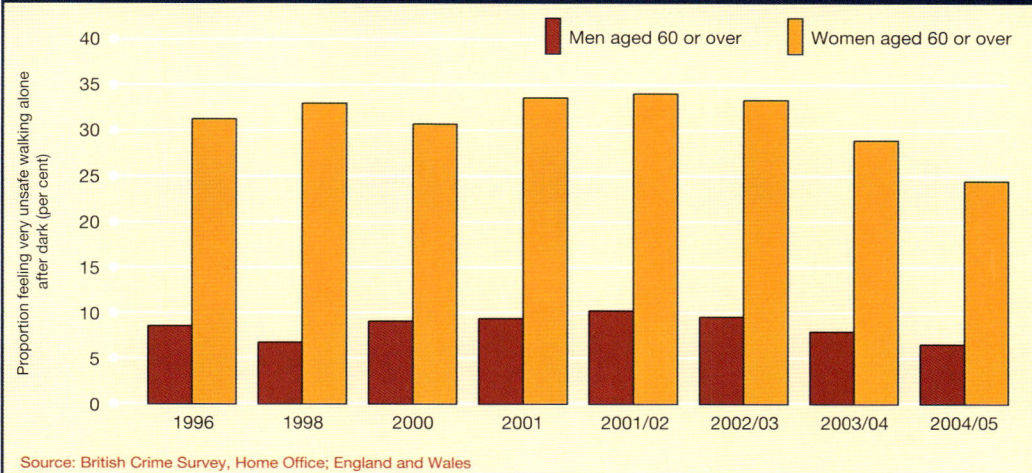

Legend: Men aged 60 or over / Women aged 60 or over

Y-axis: Proportion feeling very unsafe walking alone after dark (per cent)

X-axis categories: 1996, 1998, 2000, 2001, 2001/02, 2002/03, 2003/04, 2004/05

Source: British Crime Survey, Home Office; England and Wales

43B: Among women aged 60 and over, those from lower income households are one and a half times as likely to feel very unsafe out at night as those from higher income households.

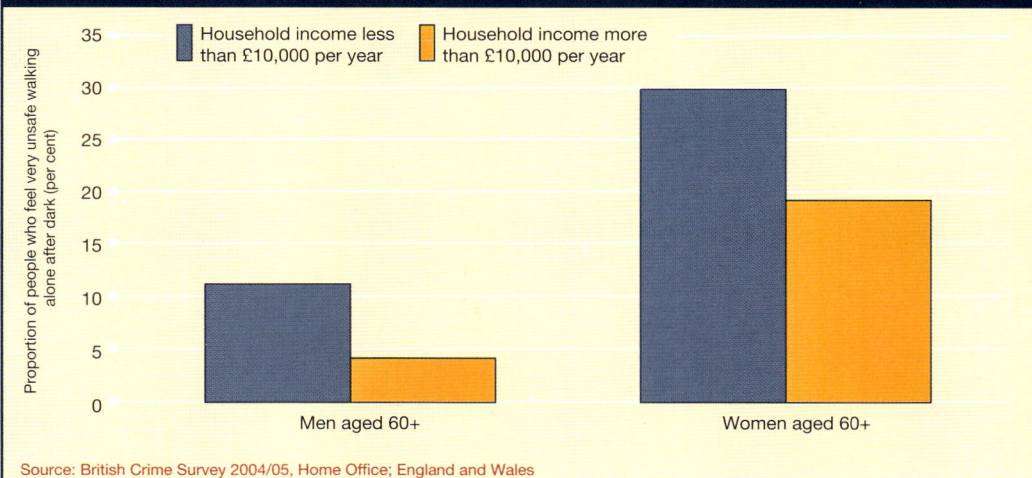

Legend: Household income less than £10,000 per year / Household income more than £10,000 per year

Y-axis: Proportion of people who feel very unsafe walking alone after dark (per cent)

X-axis categories: Men aged 60+, Women aged 60+

Source: British Crime Survey 2004/05, Home Office; England and Wales

The first graph shows the proportion of people aged 60 or over who say that they feel very unsafe walking alone in their area after dark, with the data shown separately for men and women.

The second graph shows, for the latest year, a breakdown of the statistics according to whether the people lived in households with an annual income of more or less than £10,000.

The data source for both graphs is the British Crime Survey (BCS). The data relates to England and Wales.

Overall adequacy of the indicator: medium. The BCS is a well established annual government survey and the fact that the proportions feeling very unsafe have changed little over successive surveys suggests a degree of robustness to this result. However, it is unclear to what extent these feelings reflect anxiety more generally or simply with respect to walking at night.

Chapter 6
Community

Community

This chapter has two themes containing seven indicators in total. The themes are:

■ access to services;

■ housing.

In previous years, this chapter has also contained material on neighbourhoods, crime and participation. This material is now contained in a sister report called *Housing and Neighbourhoods Monitor*, published in 2006 by the Joseph Rowntree Foundation.

Access to services

Choice of indicators

The first indicator shows the proportion of households lacking any type of bank or building society account, something which both increases the cost of utilities and can make it harder to get a job. The first graph compares the trends for low and average income households over the last decade while the second provides a further breakdown by ethnic group and economic status.

The second indicator compares the burglary rate over the last five years for households who have home contents insurance with the rate for households who do not. The first graph shows changes over time and the second shows how the proportion lacking such insurance varies according to level of household income.

The final indicator relates to cars. The first graph compares difficulties in accessing essential services for households with and without cars and the second graph shows the proportion of people without car by family type, ranging from working-age couples with children, to single pensioners.

What the indicators show

Indicator 44 Without a bank account

The proportion of low income households with no bank or building society account has fallen sharply in recent years.

Sick, disabled, unemployed and lone parent households, as well as Black, Indian, Pakistani and Bangladeshi households, are all somewhat more likely to have no account than households on average.

Indicator 45 Without home contents insurance

Households with no home contents insurance are three times as likely to be burgled as those with insurance.

Half of the poorest households do not have home contents insurance. This compares to one in five of households on average incomes.

Indicator 46 Transport

The proportion of households who find it difficult to access essential local services is much higher for those without cars than for those with cars.

Just about all couples have a car but many singles – both with and without children – do not.

Housing

Choice of indicators

The indicators in this theme cover a selected number of issues of housing for disadvantaged groups. For a much wider analysis, see the recent report called *Housing and Neighbourhoods Monitor*, published in 2006 by the Joseph Rowntree Foundation.

The first indicator presents information on the degree to which low income and workless households are concentrated in particular forms of tenure.

The second indicator shows the proportion of households lacking central heating, with the first graph comparing low and average income households over the last decade and the second graph providing a further breakdown by tenure. Lack of central heating has traditionally been considered to be one of the major reasons for energy-inefficient housing, in turn leading to potential problems of dampness, risks to health etc. As such, unlike the wider concept of 'decent homes' or the more focused concept of fuel poverty, data on central heating is available on an annual basis.

The third indicator concerns homelessness. The first graph shows how many households each year since 1997 have been accepted by their local authority as being homeless, with the data shown separately for households with and without dependent children. The supporting graph provides a breakdown by ethnic group.

The final indicator relates to insecure owner occupation. The first graph shows the number of mortgage holders in serious arrears each year starting in 1990, that is before the mortgage crisis of the early 1990s. It also shows the number of court orders made for repossession, as this shows a rather different trend to arrears in recent years. The second graph shows the number of mortgage holders with either no job or only a part-time job.

What the indicators show

Indicator 47 Polarisation by tenure

Almost half of all people in social housing are on low incomes compared to one in seven of those in other housing tenures.

Half of heads of households aged between 25 and 54 in social rented housing are not in paid work compared to just one in twenty of those in owner occupation.

Indicator 48 Without central heating

Although poorer households remain more likely to lack central heating, the proportion who do so is now actually less than that for households on average incomes in 1999/2000.

Those living in the private rented sector are the most likely to be without central heating.

Indicator 49 Homelessness

The number of newly homeless households fell sharply in 2005, but was still 150,000 households.

A quarter of those accepted as homeless and in priority need by English local authorities are from minority ethnic groups.

Indicator 50 In mortgage arrears

While the number of mortgage holders in serious arrears remains very low, court orders for repossession are now back to their levels of a decade ago.

One in seven working-age heads of households with a mortgage is in an economically vulnerable position – in part-time work, unemployed or economically inactive.

Without a bank account

44A: The proportion of low income households with no bank or building society account has fallen sharply in recent years.

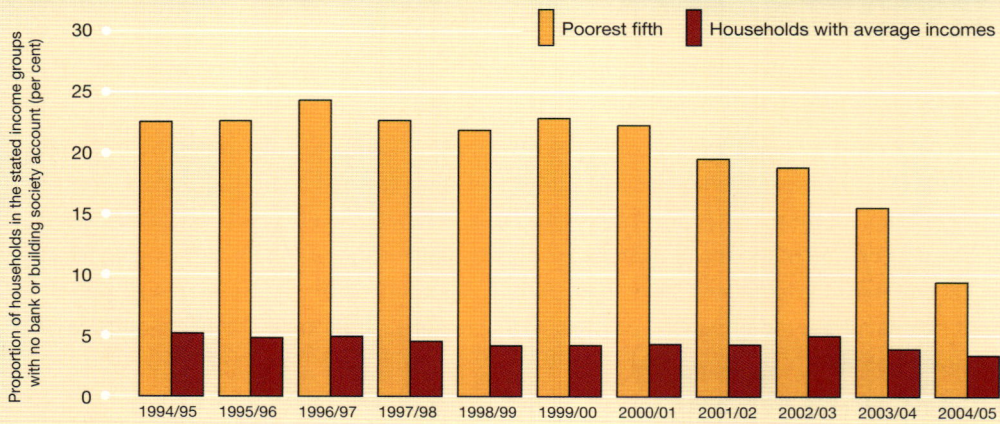

Poorest fifth | Households with average incomes

Y-axis: Proportion of households in the stated income groups with no bank or building society account (per cent)

X-axis: 1994/95, 1995/96, 1996/97, 1997/98, 1998/99, 1999/00, 2000/01, 2001/02, 2002/03, 2003/04, 2004/05

Source: Family Resources Survey, DWP; GB

44B: Sick, disabled, unemployed and lone parent households, as well as Black, Indian, Pakistani and Bangladeshi households, are all somewhat more likely to have no account than households on average.

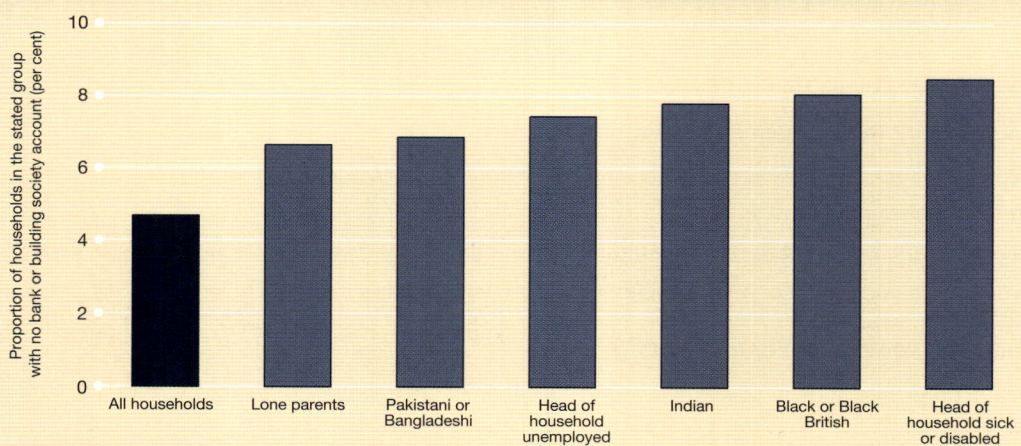

Y-axis: Proportion of households in the stated group with no bank or building society account (per cent)

X-axis: All households, Lone parents, Pakistani or Bangladeshi, Head of household unemployed, Indian, Black or Black British, Head of household sick or disabled

Source: Family Resources Survey 2004/05, DWP; UK

The first graph shows the proportion of households without a bank, building society or any other kind of account. The data is split to show separately households in the poorest fifth of the income distribution and households on average incomes. Income is household disposable income, equivalised (adjusted) to take account of household composition, and is measured after deducting housing costs.

The second graph shows how the proportions in the latest year vary for selected different household types, as determined by the head of the household. A figure for all households is provided for comparison.

The data source for both graphs is the Family Resources Survey (FRS). The data relates to Great Britain in the first graph and to the United Kingdom in the second graph (FRS did not cover Northern Ireland before 2002/03). As well as bank, building society and post office accounts, the figures also count any savings or investment accounts but do not include stocks and shares, premium bonds, gilts or Save As You Earn arrangements.

Overall adequacy of the indicator: high. FRS is probably the most representative of the surveys that gather information on the extent to which people have bank and other types of account.

Without home contents insurance

45A: Households with no home contents insurance are three times as likely to be burgled as those with insurance.

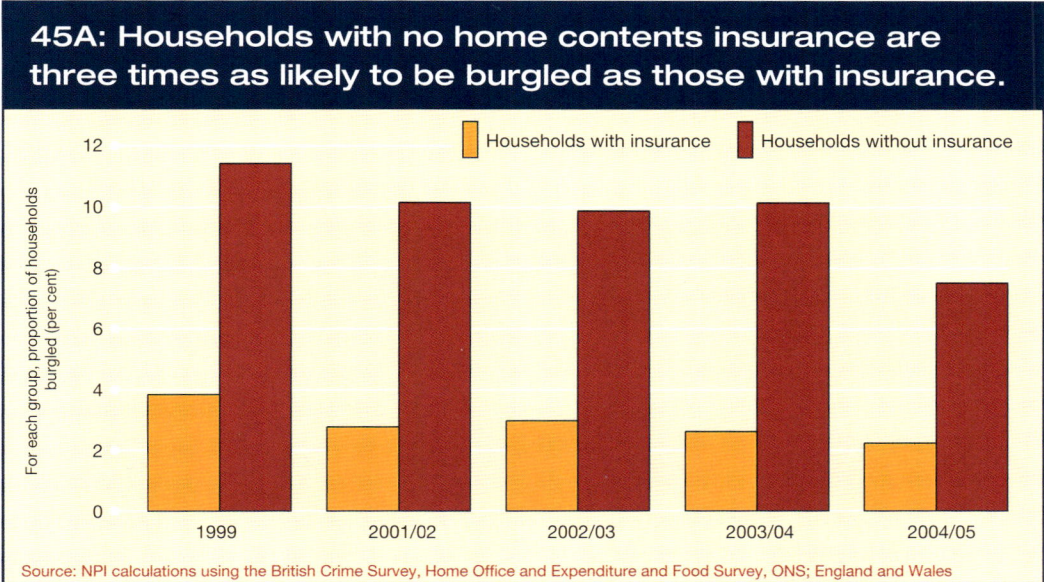

Legend: ■ Households with insurance   ■ Households without insurance

Y-axis: For each group, proportion of households burgled (per cent); scale 0 to 12

X-axis: 1999, 2001/02, 2002/03, 2003/04, 2004/05

Source: NPI calculations using the British Crime Survey, Home Office and Expenditure and Food Survey, ONS; England and Wales

45B: Half of the poorest households do not have home contents insurance. This compares to one in five for households on average incomes.

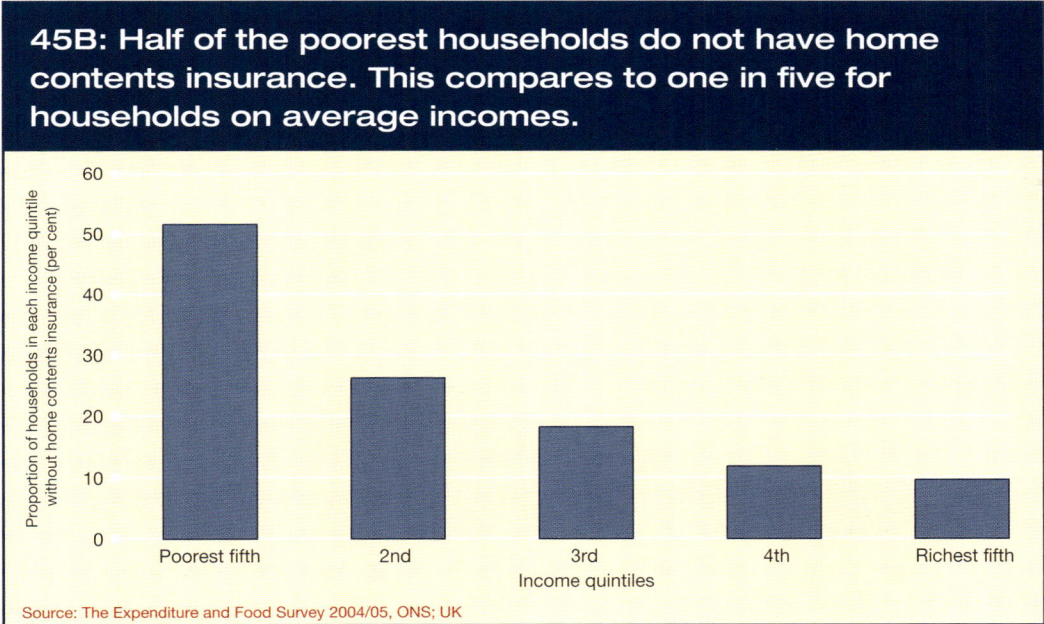

Y-axis: Proportion of households in each income quintile without home contents insurance (per cent); scale 0 to 60

X-axis: Poorest fifth, 2nd, 3rd, 4th, Richest fifth — Income quintiles

Source: The Expenditure and Food Survey 2004/05, ONS; UK

The first graph shows the proportion of households with, and without, home contents insurance that were victims of a burglary one or more times in each of the years shown. The rate is calculated by the New Policy Institute using data on burglaries from the British Crime Survey (BCS) and data on household insurance from the Expenditure and Food Survey (EFS). The estimates are for England and Wales. Note that data for years earlier than 1999 has not been included in the graph as it was collected on a different basis (via a direct question in the BCS) and is therefore not directly comparable.

The second graph shows, for the latest year, how the proportion of households without insurance cover for household contents varies according to the household's income . The division into income quintiles is based on gross, equivalised (adjusted for household size) income. The data source is EFS and relates to the United Kingdom.

Overall adequacy of the indicator: medium. The BCS and EFS are well-established government surveys, which are designed to be nationally representative.

Transport

46A: The proportion of households who find it difficult to access essential local services is much higher for those without cars than for those with cars.

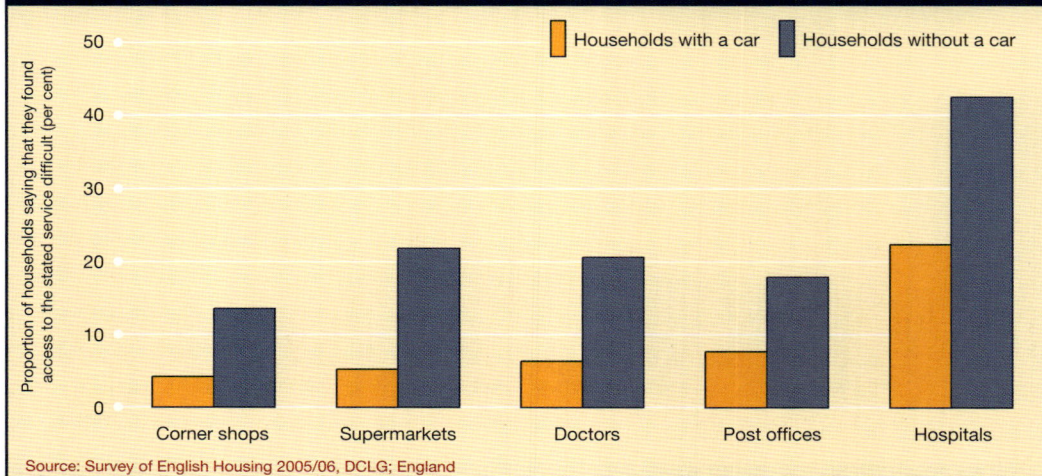

Proportion of households saying that they found access to the stated service difficult (per cent)

Legend: Households with a car | Households without a car

Categories: Corner shops, Supermarkets, Doctors, Post offices, Hospitals

Source: Survey of English Housing 2005/06, DCLG; England

46B: Just about all couples have a car but many singles – both with and without children – do not.

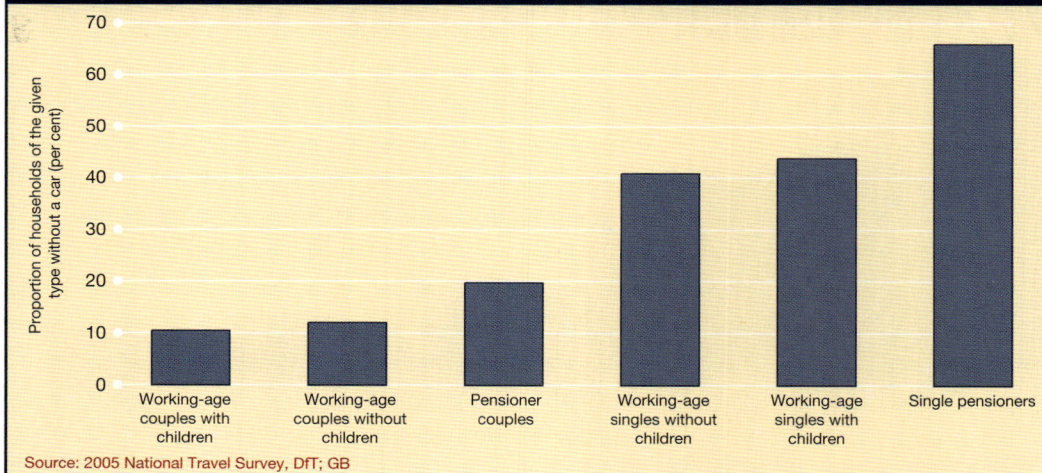

Proportion of households of the given type without a car (per cent)

Categories: Working-age couples with children, Working-age couples without children, Pensioner couples, Working-age singles without children, Working-age singles with children, Single pensioners

Source: 2005 National Travel Survey, DfT; GB

The first graph shows the proportion of households who say that they find it difficult to access a selection of essential local services, with the data shown separately for households with and without cars. The data source is the Survey of English Housing. The data is for 2005/06 and is for England only.

The second graph shows the proportion of households who do not have access to either a car or van, with the data shown separately for each major type of household. The data source is the 2004 National Travel Survey and the data relates to Great Britain. Households are classified as working-age or pensioner depending on whether the household reference person is aged 65+ or not.

Overall adequacy of the indicator: medium. The data comes from well-established annual government surveys, designed to be nationally representative, but only covers one aspect of transport.

Polarisation by tenure

47A: Almost half of all people in social housing are on low incomes compared to one in seven of those in other housing tenures.

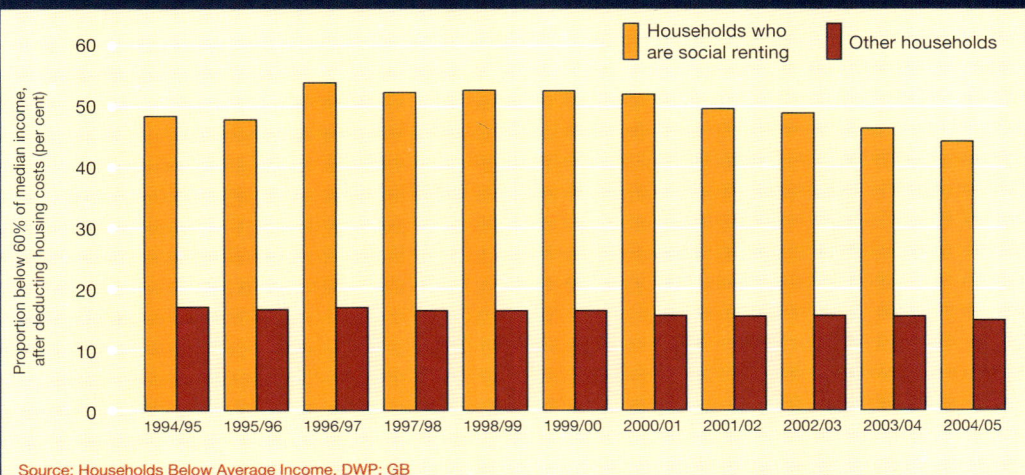

Households who are social renting ■ Other households

Proportion below 60% of median income, after deducting housing costs (per cent)

Source: Households Below Average Income, DWP; GB

47B: Half of heads of households aged between 25 and 54 in social rented housing are not in paid work compared to just one in twenty of those in owner-occupation.

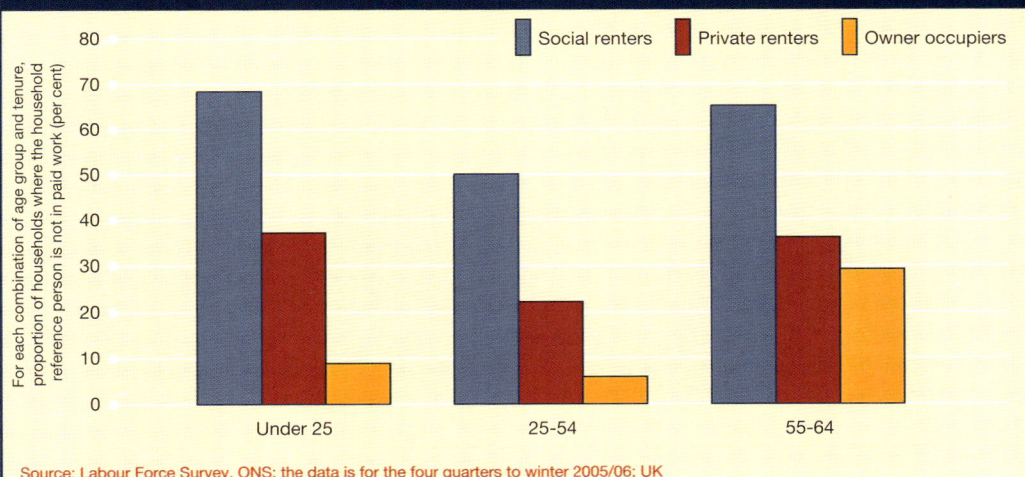

■ Social renters ■ Private renters ■ Owner occupiers

For each combination of age group and tenure, proportion of households where the household reference person is not in paid work (per cent)

Under 25   25-54   55-64

Source: Labour Force Survey, ONS; the data is for the four quarters to winter 2005/06; UK

The first graph shows the proportion of people in low income households for people in social housing compared to people in other housing tenures. The data source is Households Below Average Income, based on the Family Resources Survey (FRS). The data relates to Great Britain. Income is disposable household income after deducting housing costs and the low income threshold is the same as that used elsewhere, namely 60 per cent of median household income. All data is equivalised (adjusted) to account for variation in household size and composition. The self-employed are included in the calculations.

The second graph shows, for 2005/06, the proportion of working-age households where the 'household reference person' (which is the person with the highest income in the household) is not in paid work, with the data broken down by age group and tenure. The data source is the Labour Force Survey and the data relates to the United Kingdom.

Overall adequacy of the indicator: high. The FRS is a well-established annual government survey, designed to be representative of the population as a whole.

Without central heating

48A: Although poorer households remain more likely to lack central heating, the proportion who do so is now actually less than that for households on average incomes in 1999/00.

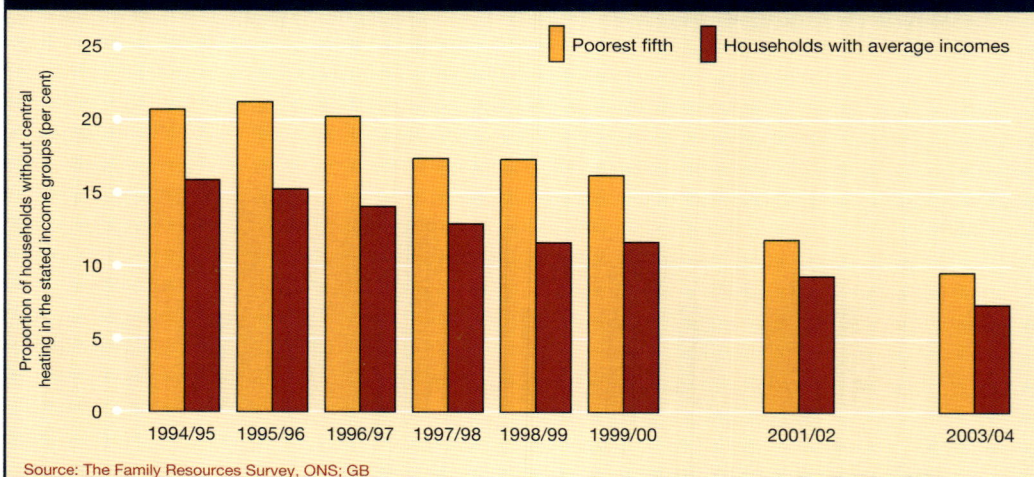

Legend: Poorest fifth; Households with average incomes

Y-axis: Proportion of households without central heating in the stated income groups (per cent)

X-axis: 1994/95, 1995/96, 1996/97, 1997/98, 1998/99, 1999/00, 2001/02, 2003/04

Source: The Family Resources Survey, ONS; GB

48B: Those living in the private rented sector are the most likely to be without central heating.

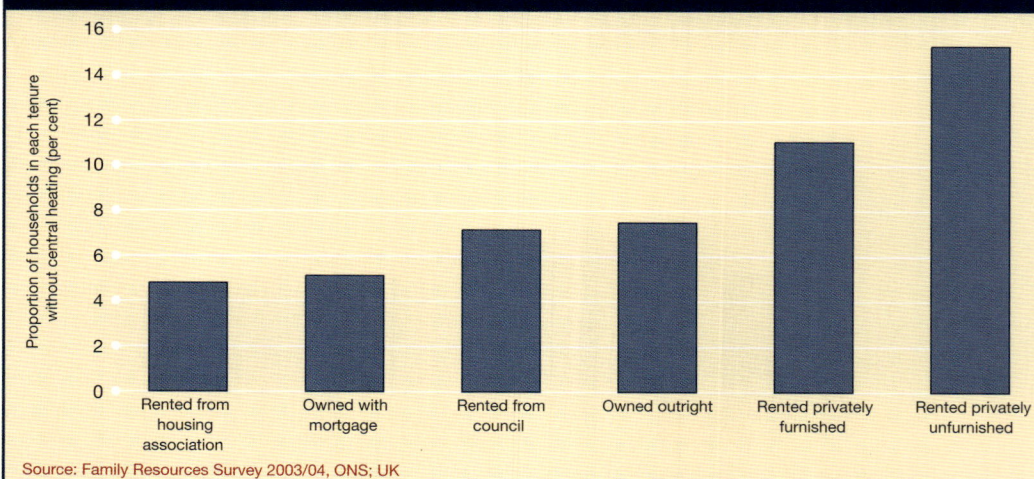

Y-axis: Proportion of households in each tenure without central heating (per cent)

X-axis: Rented from housing association, Owned with mortgage, Rented from council, Owned outright, Rented privately furnished, Rented privately unfurnished

Source: Family Resources Survey 2003/04, ONS; UK

The first graph shows the proportion of households without central heating. The data is split to show households in the poorest fifth of the income distribution and households on average incomes (middle fifth of the income distribution) separately. Income is household disposable income, equivalised (adjusted) to take account of household composition, and is measured after deducting housing costs.

The second graph shows, for the latest year, how the proportion varies by housing tenure.

The data source for both graphs is the Family Resources Survey (FRS). The data relates to Great Britain in the first graph and to the United Kingdom in the second graph (FRS did not cover Northern Ireland prior to 2002/03). The missing years in the first graph are because the question about central heating is only asked in some years. Also note that the question was not asked in 2004/05.

Overall adequacy of the indicator: high. The FRS is a well-established, regular government survey, designed to be nationally representative.

Homelessness

49A: The number of newly homeless households fell sharply in 2005, but was still 150,000 households.

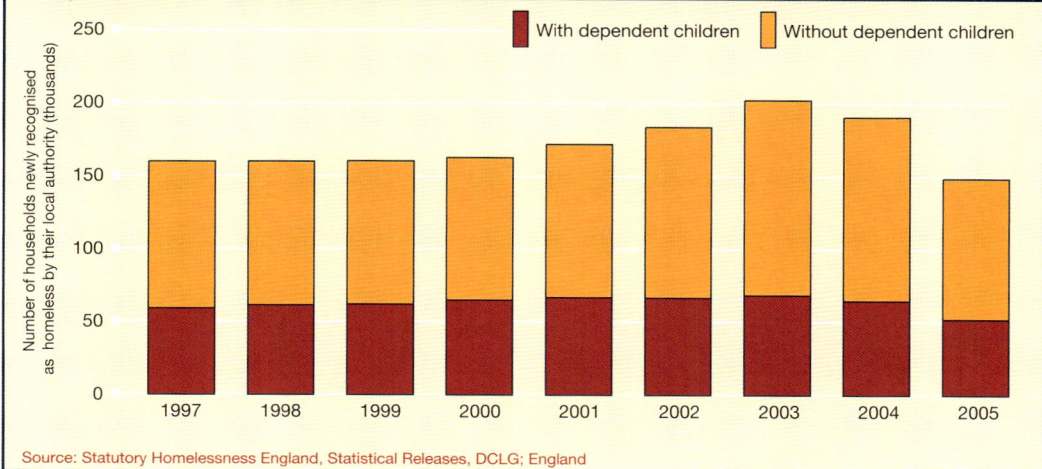

Legend: With dependent children / Without dependent children

Y-axis: Number of households newly recognised as homeless by their local authority (thousands)

Source: Statutory Homelessness England, Statistical Releases, DCLG; England

49B: A quarter of those accepted as homeless and in priority need by English local authorities are from ethnic minorities.

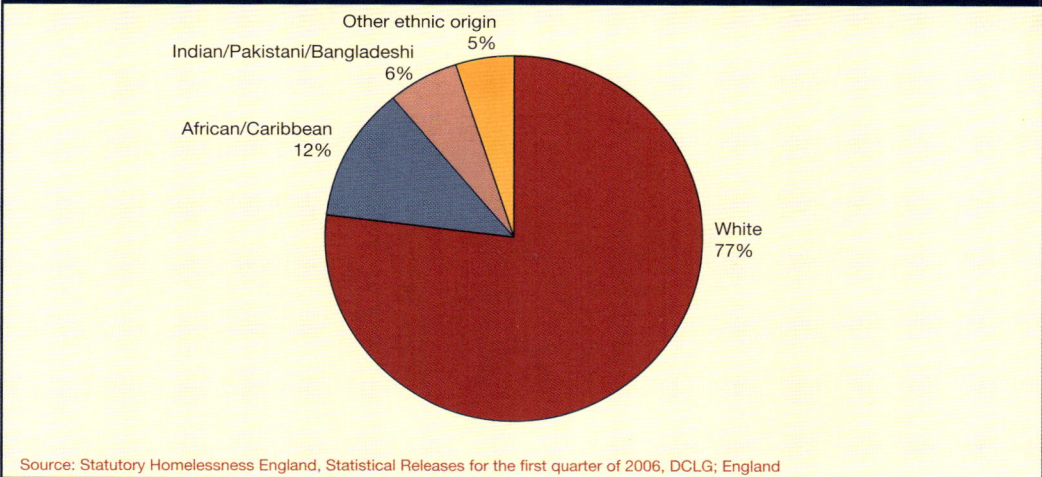

- Other ethnic origin 5%
- Indian/Pakistani/Bangladeshi 6%
- African/Caribbean 12%
- White 77%

Source: Statutory Homelessness England, Statistical Releases for the first quarter of 2006, DCLG; England

The first graph shows the number of households in England who were accepted as homeless by their local authority in each of the stated years, with the data split between those with and without dependent children. It includes both those 'in priority need' and those 'not in priority need' but excludes those deemed to be intentionally homeless (a relatively small number) as division by family type is not available for this group. In line with the Department for Communities and Local Government (DCLG) guidance, the numbers with children are assumed to be the same as the numbers who are in priority need because they have children. Scotland and Wales are not included in this graph because the legislative environment is different.

The second graph provides, for the first quarter of 2006, a breakdown by ethnic group of the households that were accepted by local authorities in England as being homeless and 'in priority need' (no equivalent statistics are kept for those 'not in priority need').

The data source for both graphs is the DCLG Statutory Homelessness England, Statistical Releases.

Overall adequacy of the indicator: medium. While there is no reason to believe there is any problem with the underlying data, it leaves 'homelessness' dependent on administrative judgement which is not satisfactory. In particular, the figures do not include many single people who are effectively homeless, as local authorities have no general duty to house such people and therefore many do not apply.

In mortgage arrears

50A: While the number of mortgage holders in serious arrears remains very low, court orders for repossession are now back to their levels of a decade ago.

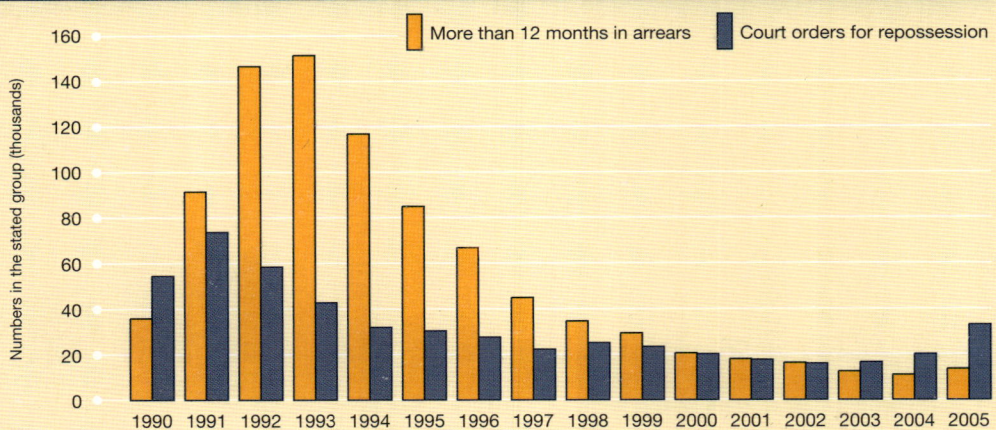

Legend: More than 12 months in arrears / Court orders for repossession

Y-axis: Numbers in the stated group (thousands)

Source: Council of Mortgage Lenders and Department for Constitutional Affairs; UK

50B: One in seven working-age heads of households with a mortgage is in an economically vulnerable position – in part-time work, unemployed or economically inactive.

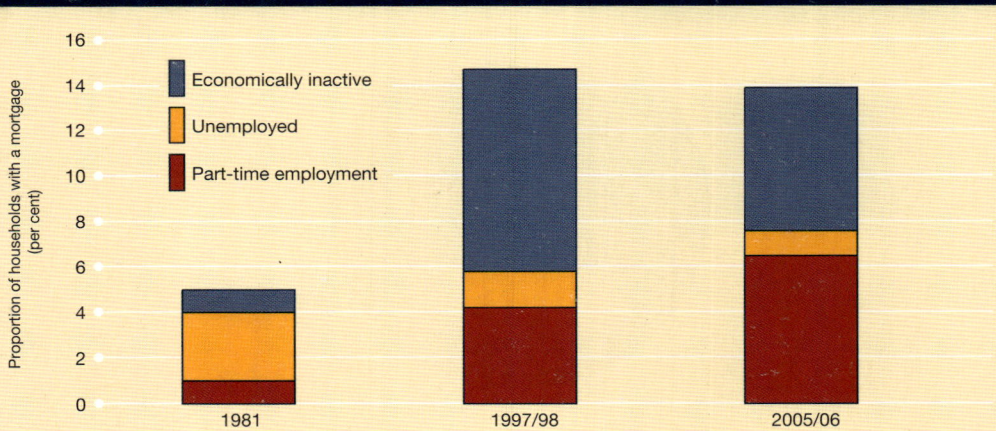

Legend: Economically inactive / Unemployed / Part-time employment

Y-axis: Proportion of households with a mortgage (per cent)

X-axis: 1981, 1997/98, 2005/06

Source: LFS Housing Trailer, DoE (1981); Survey of English Housing, DCLG (1997/98 and 2005/06); England

The first graph shows both the number of residential mortgage holders who were 12 months or more in arrears with their mortgage repayments at the end of each of the years shown and the number of court orders made for mortgage repossession during each year. Note the number of orders excludes suspended orders, as these do not directly relate to repossessions.

The data source for mortgage arrears is the Council of Mortgage Lenders (CML) and relates to the United Kingdom. The figures are based on a sample which typically averages 85 per cent of the total mortgage market in any given year. The data source for court orders is the UK Housing Review table 53, which in turn obtained its data from the Department for Constitutional Affairs (DCA); the data relates to England and Wales.

The second graph shows the proportion of households with mortgages where the head of the household has the economic status shown. The data is from the Survey of English Housing and relates to England only.

Overall adequacy of the indicator: high. The data for both arrears and court orders is produced regularly and is considered to be reliable.